Battleground ~~Europe~~

GALLIPOLI:
THE LANDINGS AT HELLES

Battleground Europe

GALLIPOLI: THE LANDINGS AT HELLES

Huw & Jill Rodge

Series editor
Nigel Cave

LEO COOPER

DEDICATION

To
All those who fought,
All who survived
And all who still remain on the Peninsula

Vixere fortes ante Agamemnona
Multi: sed omnes illacrimabiles
Urgentur ignotique longa
Nocte, crent quia vate sacro   Horace
The story of gallant deeds should be told before it is too late

Before Atrides men were brave
But ah: oblivion, dark and long
Has locked them in a tearless grave
For lack of consecrating song.
Conington's translation from Odes, Book IV, No. 9

First published in 2003 by
LEO COOPER
an imprint of
Pen & Sword Books Limited
47 Church Street, Barnsley, South Yorkshire S70 2AS

Copyright © Huw & Jill Rodge

ISBN 1 84415 009 7

A CIP catalogue of this book is available
from the British Library

Printed by CPI UK

For up-to-date information on other titles produced under the Leo Cooper imprint,
please telephone or write to:

Pen & Sword Books Ltd, FREEPOST, 47 Church Street
Barnsley, South Yorkshire S70 2AS
Telephone 01226 734222

CONTENTS

Introduction by Series Editor... **6**

Author's Introduction.. **7**

Advice to Tourers... **10**

Orientation – Car Tour... **18**

Chapter 1 **Why Did it Happen? The Dardanelles up to 1915**............ **25**

Chapter 2 **Y Beach – and what might have been**............................ **43**

           Walk One.. **59**

Chapter 3 **X Beach – A defiant stand**... **64**

           Walk Two.. **76**

Chapter 4 **W Beach – Six Victoria Crosses before breakfast**............ **80**

           Walk Three.. **109**

Chapter 5 **V Beach – Carnage and courage**................................... **119**

           Walk Four.. **155**

Chapter 6 **S Beach – Success at last**.. **166**

           Walk Five.. **181**

Chapter 7 **Feint Attacks**... **185**

Afterthought.. **187**

Select Bibliography and Recommended Reading............................ **189**

Selective index... **190**

Acknowledgements.. **192**

INTRODUCTION BY SERIES EDITOR

The landings at Gallipoli were the biggest amphibious assault ever attempted in history up to that time. The consequence of a 'quick fix' naval assault that failed was to lead to the Gallipoli campaign that only lasted just over eight months, but it has had a peculiar resonance to those who have followed all these years afterwards.

Today Gallipoli, particularly the Helles beaches, is generally an extremely solitary place – it is easy to wander around all day on parts of the battlefield and see hardly another human being. Today's visitor here (and to a lesser extent on much of the Somme, Arras and Cambrai battlefields) can only be struck by the contrast of the beauty and silence of the present contrasted with the carnage and brutality of then.

Helles, however, has a particular quality; a beautiful sea, largely empty beaches (with one or two notable exceptions, and even these are not truly busy), an area steeped in ancient history, an almost biblical landscape, wonderful natural life – and then the tragedy of the events of 1915. The land campaign began here, and the heroism displayed on that day – undoubtedly by men of both sides – was, and is, inspirational. I have spent several weeks on the peninsula, most of it staying in a *pension* just above V Beach and within a few minutes walk of the redoubtable Lieutenant Colonel Doughty-Wylie's grave. My time here was an experience that is one that will doubtless remain for a lifetime.

There are now some excellent guides to Gallipoli, but it is hoped that this latest one in the *Battleground Europe* series on the peninsula will add considerably to a visit to the tragic beaches of Helles.

Nigel Cave
Porta Latina, Rome. 2003.

INTRODUCTION

'Who is to have Constantinople?' wrote Napoleon two years after Trafalgar. He continued: 'If Russia controls the Dardanelles she will be at the gates of Toulon, Naples and Corfu'.

Today Turkey is recognised as an attractive holiday destination but speak to the British about the problems in Gallipoli in 1915, and doubt creeps in to the conversation. On a recent U.K. quiz show with University graduates, not one member of either team knew the location of Gallipoli. Not so of course with our Australian friends who flock there in their thousands every year, particularly on Anzac Day, 25th April.

It has become a 'forgotten war' for the British, and those who fought and died there under such grim and trying conditions may soon be forgotten. Thousands lie there still, many in unmarked graves. This view is accentuated each time we visit the Peninsula. On more than one of our frequent visits, Australians have queried the reason why we, as British citizens, are on Gallipoli and express curiosity as to why we are interested in what, to them, is considered to be an Australian campaign. They are more than surprised to learn that the British had the dubious distinction of suffering more fatal casualties than the Australians and New Zealanders together. The lovely beaches and quiet cemeteries at

Aerial view Helles – January 1916. (Courtesy of Royal Navy Submarine Museum)

Helles do not attract so many visitors by comparison with the thousands of young backpackers from the Southern Hemisphere who visit the Anzac areas, but it is our hope that this book, with its stories of great courage and self-sacrifice, will in some small way remedy this.

The Dardanelles have always attracted attention as being an intrinsic part of the direct water way between France and Russia in the Mediterranean, so important when the northern ports of Russia are icebound. It is the only entrance and exit of the Aegean to the Black Sea, the doorway to Russia with the mouths of great rivers such as the Danube and the Don and ports including Constantinople, Odessa and Sebastopol

The aim of this book, is to give a reasonably detailed account of the Landings at Helles on the southern tip of the Gallipoli Peninsula in April of 1915, and the immediate aftermath of those landings, together with a description of the ground and the possibility of visiting such areas, with routes for walking and a car tour.

Little has really changed today from all those years ago, unlike the battlefields of France and Belgium, and little is likely to, either, as the area has been declared to be a National Park. It is now also possible to visit most of the locations and areas involved in the Campaign, due to the lifting of military restrictions.

It is indeed salutary to visit the Peninsula and remember those officers and men of all nationalities who fought in extreme temperatures – scorching sun, debilitating dysentery, disgusting flies and lice, as well as heavy rainfall, unexpected and dangerous flooding, bitter cold, ice and snow. So many who died so far away from home and those they loved, rest today in beautifully kept cemeteries maintained by the dedication of the Commonwealth War Graves Commission that look so different from those in Western Europe and have a haunting ethos of their own.

In 1994 an immense fire broke out on the Peninsula and thousands of trees in over 4000 hectares of land were destroyed. It was of course disastrous from an ecological and aesthetic point of view, and involved sad loss of life, which was very regrettable. But it did enable one for a short while to visit the battlefield areas and see it as the boys would have experienced it, ie without the huge fir trees and other growth, some over 30 years old, the result of a re-afforestation scheme by the Turks. We were able to find original trenchlines, black and scorched, a little easier than before, and views were extensive. For example, standing at Lone Pine one could see clearly see the area of the Nek and Chanuk Bair and the view down towards Helles.

An International Peace Park is being established on the Peninsula

1. General Map.

St Sophia, Istanbul.

and hopefully will curtail new building work and excessive afforestation as well as the erection of new memorials of which there has been a surfeit over the past years.

Finally we would like to add that our book is not intended to be either a political or a military critique but rather a detailed account of the actions at Helles on 25 April and subsequent events until the end of 27 April, 1915, which hopefully will go some way to assist the reader in exploring the Gallipoli Peninsula, following in the footsteps of those brave souls who landed and fought at Helles in some of the most dangerous and most miserable battlefield conditions of the First World War, and finally to help us all in

'KEEPING ALIVE THE MEMORY'

ADVICE TO TOURERS

The battlefields of the Gallipoli Peninsula are in many respects quite different to the more familiar lanes, woods and valleys of the Somme or the flat, often muddy, fields and tracks of the Ypres Salient. A visit will entail some forward planning as it is a longer and relatively expensive journey.

Turkey, with its centuries of fascinating archaeological, literary and military history, is an exciting and very different country to visit, with important and interesting cultural differences. Today it is a major popular holiday destination. Istanbul is a vibrant and colourful city, steeped in atmosphere and it would be worthwhile to consider including a few extra days to explore its varied aspects.

Young regrowth after the fire in 1994 (from Farm Cemetery).

It is still possible virtually to have the Peninsula to oneself, if the significant anniversary dates for both the Allies and the Turks are avoided. Whilst the ceremonies are very important and emotive, their very nature means the area can be very crowded, noisy and accommodation needs to be booked well in advance. Away from this period one can explore at leisure, taking one's time to discover original trench lines, walk the ground, reflect on all that took place and find a cool drink at the end of the day and relax.

As with any study of a military action, it is helpful to do some background reading, particularly if one is aware of the involvement of a relative. It does avoid the frustrated and anguished cry we have heard so many times 'if only I had found out about that before I came!' Any time spent in preparation beforehand is never wasted.

Trenches at Lone Pine.

On the practical side, a good guidebook, with maps, a compass, a pair of binoculars – useful not just for the battlefields but for the birdlife present – a camera and supply of film (although it is possible to purchase some in Cannakale or Eceabat now) are recommended. Strong walking boots and a windproof jacket are essential. Whilst there are chemists in Cannakale we would suggest that if you need to take medication, bring a sufficient supply with you to last the visit. Full

11

Café scene, Cannakale.   **Be prepared.**

personal medical and health insurance is important, as well as cover for loss and theft of your belongings. If you are tempted to touch rusty remains such as barbed wire, shells or bullets that can be found lying round, a tetanus jab would be advised. It is, however, a criminal offence and forbidden by the Gallipoli National Park and the Turkish Government to take away any such objects. Doing so also spoils it for other visitors that follow.

It should be borne in mind that the Gallipoli Peninsula becomes extremely hot normally from mid-May to early September and a hat, sunglasses and suntan lotion are essential, together with insect repellent. We have visited in early spring when it can be cold and windy; and also in winter, with the battlefields covered in snow, so one should be prepared for inclement weather conditions. On one visit the authors nearly missed their plane due to sudden unexpected heavy snowfall in the hills between Cannakale and Istanbul!

If you plan to walk off the beaten track it is suggested you take a companion with you and a mobile telephone (with the local emergency number to contact in case of difficulty). Whilst the ground at Helles is not quite so rough or difficult to explore compared with other parts of the Peninsula, it is possible to twist a knee or ankle quite easily and a stick is useful. Take a simple picnic – fresh bread, cheese and fruit is available in Krithia (Alcitepe) for example, together with the essential

Battefield artefacts in private museum, Alcitepe (Krithia).

bottle of water. If for no other reason, a snack could be useful for bribing the packs of stray dogs roaming around, particularly near the Gully Ravine/Pink Farm area. The author gained a well deserved reputation at Lala Baba on one recent occasion by pacifying a large dog's threatening behaviour and thereby saving his group from an uncertain fate!

Walking in the north of the Peninsula, particularly around the Chanuk Bair area, is a more serious matter, especially if you are walking along the various deres (stream beds) that reach from the summits down to the coastline. We would strongly recommend a compass and some basic skills in map reading.

Various forms of wildlife can be seen, including terrapins, tortoises, jackals and snakes, the latter normally seen in the bush around Chanuk Bair. Many different kinds of birds are present, including

Specimens of local animal life, some more friendly than others.

the spectacular bee-eaters at Kum Kale.

If a UK citizen, a full 10 year British passport is required and at present it is necessary to purchase a 3 month entry visa at Passport Control on landing with **sterling** (£10) or at a border post. It is possible to obtain Turkish lira from the airports or the banks in Cannakale, which is useful for small purchases, cups of coffee etc.

Getting there

If you decide to visit the Peninsula with a group, there are specialist military history organisations who will make the necessary arrangements for you. For independent travellers, there are regular flights to Istanbul International Airport, with Izmir on the coast as an alternative venue, both from the UK and other major European cities. On arrival, you have four main alternative methods of reaching the Gallipoli Peninsula.

1. Taxi

This is a more expensive enterprise. Please note that for long journeys and for a few days hire, payment in US$ cash is preferred. The journey from the airport to Cannakale, including the crossing by ferryboat, takes between 5 and 6 hours. It is advisable to agree a price before commencing your journey.

2. Car Hire from Istanbul

This is another option which would need to be arranged in advance. Most major car hire companies are represented. A full current driving licence would be required. The main drawback is that one would have to negotiate the horrendous traffic and constant diversions around the airport and city of Istanbul, mainly due to building works, which can be nerve wracking to say the least, and then cope with some indifferent roads down to the Peninsula! Laws are similar to mainland Europe – you drive on the right and seat belts have to be worn.

3. Coach

Turkey has an excellent and reliable coach network which goes to many destinations in the country from Istanbul – a big plus point is that they run on time! The main bus station (Otopark) is about 20 minutes by taxi or shuttle bus from Istanbul International Airport. Whilst it can be daunting to ensure that you get on the right bus as the choice is vast,

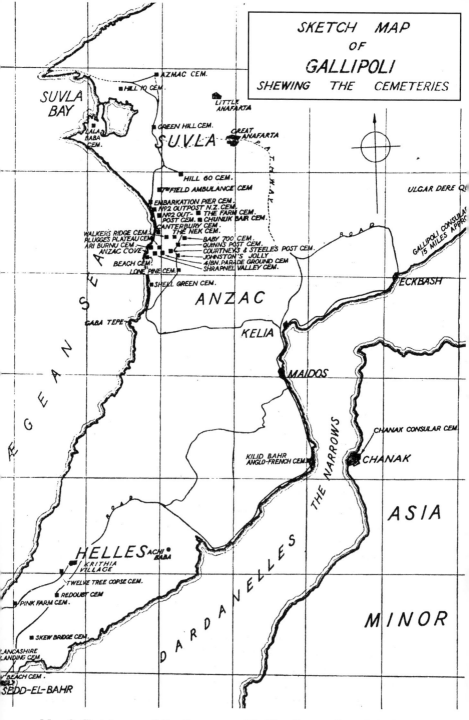

Map 2. Sketch map of the Commonwealth War Graves Commission's cemeteries, Gallipoli.

the luxury coach with hostess on board will take about 5/6 hours to Cannakale. There are hot drinks on board and comfort stops en route, where basic toilet facilities (one pays a small charge) and snacks can also be purchased.

Out and about
Once in either Cannakale or Eceabat, unless you book a tour with a local travel agency or are young and extremely fit, you will find that transport of some kind is required to visit the battlefields.

It is possible to hire a car, motorbike or bicycle in Cannakale from Gezgin Rent a Car, just a few minutes walk from the port, at No. 2a Cumhuriyet Meydani Tekki Sk., Tel: +(90) 286 212 8392. A deposit may be required. You can also check at the local Tourist Office near the Ferry Terminal for other hire companies Tel: +(90) 286 217 11187.

Maps
It is still difficult to obtain modern detailed maps of the Peninsula. The maps in this book should assist the battlefield visitor. In addition the Gallipoli Peninsula National Historical Park have produced an interesting map. The CWGC have also produced a map which shows the site of all their cemeteries and memorials and is available from their offices in Maidenhead. It would also be remiss of us not to mention our good friends Major and Mrs. Toni and Valmai Holt who have published an excellent map, which can be purchased separately from their guide book to Gallipoli.

Accommodation
Cannakale is a busy, bustling and very colourful port, with its fishing boats, tugs, and the huge car ferries plying their way across the Narrows. It has a pleasant atmosphere, with simple waterfront cafes and restaurants, friendly and helpful service and the port itself heaves with activity in this thriving community. Small shops sell everything from runny orange marmalade to expensive carpets. Various travel agencies, coach companies, the local Tourist Office, PTT telephone kiosk, taxi rank, small market and several banks are all close to the ferry dock, whilst the main Police Station and Hospital are a little further inland, past Republic Square with its imposing statue of Kemal Attaturk and some Turkish guns.

The Cannakale CWGC Cemetery is well worth a visit (as it is kept locked a key is available from the local CWGC office). There is also a Military/Naval Museum at Cimenlik Fort with exhibits of the

1915 campaign. There is a wooden model of the mine-layer Nusret, the original of which wreaked such havoc in the March naval attack.

There is a choice of different types of accommodation in Cannakale, eg:

Hotel Akol (4 star) For the well heeled! Tel: +90 286 217 9456

Hotel Truva (3 star) (Ask for Salih Yukcel) Often used by the authors. Courteous, friendly, comfortable en suite rooms, some with wonderful views of the Dardanelles and the Peninsula. Welcomes battlefield visitors. Tel: +90 286 217 1024

Hotel Anafartala (3 star) Next to ferry terminal. Tel: +90 286 217 4454

Anzac House (1 star) Basic and clean, very popular with young Australians and New Zealander backpackers. Around 25 April (Anzac Day) it might mean a sleeping bag in a corridor and struggling for hot water/toilets, but great atmosphere.

Eceabat (Maidos)
A ferry ride either from the large car ferry or the smaller, quicker (and cheaper) car ferry at Cannakale takes you across to Eceabat in about 20 – 30 minutes. Simpler, more basic, accommodation is available here on the waterfront, such as the Hotel Eceabat or the Hotel Boss. Meals are available in various local cafes and tavernas. The Cannakale Tourist Office can assist with other suggestions. There are small supermarkets, fruit stalls, a taxi rank and travel agencies around the square opposite the ferry terminal. The Eceabat Down Under Travel Agency is well established and helpful. Tel: +90 286 814 2431 e-mail: d.under@excite.com.

Kum Motel and Campsite (near Gaba Tepe on the way to Helles) is an excellent complex in its own shady gardens, swimming pool, restaurant/café and direct access to sandy beach. Also there is a campsite with its own facilities, olive trees for shade. Own transport essential. Tel: +90 286 814 1455

Sedd El Bahr
The main village at Helles, with basic village cafes and shop and some simple pensions.
Helles Panorama Pansiyon – close to W and V Beaches, lovely views, with good food and very clean. Own transport necessary. Tel/Fax: +90 286 862 0035

At the end of each Chapter of this book a walking tour is described, with the suggestion of starting points from either Krithia (Alcitepe) or Sedd El Bahr. The numbers on the relevant maps indicate the approximate position of the sites mentioned.

Each beach is described separately with particular reference to the landings on 25 April 1915 and an initial orientation tour is included in the book to enable the visitor to adjust their bearings and plan their subsequent visits to the various beaches. Whilst it is possible to drive onto S Beach, the other beaches require a short walk with only some practical difficulties.

Only the briefest of details are given on the Cemeteries so it would be well worthwhile to obtain the respective Cemetery Registers from the CWGC in Maidenhead and take time to study the details at leisure before your visit.

ORIENTATION TOUR

It would be beneficial that, in order to appreciate the situation in 1915, an initial inspection be made of the ground.

For example a car tour of the southern tip of the Gallipoli Peninsula could start in either Cannakale by the Ferry Port or in **Eceabat (1)** and should take the best part of a day. It should be borne in mind that cycling around the Peninsula would take a great deal longer, and walking the whole Peninsula would be a luxury. The distance covered by this circular trip is about 70 kms and, apart from Krithia and Sedd El Bahr, the two principal villages at the toe of the Peninsula, incorporates the British landing beaches of Y, X, W, V and S. Detailed explanations of what happened at these locations will be found in the Walking Tour section at the end of each relevant chapter.

You can buy ferry tickets at Cannakale port – bear in mind that the

The bustling port of Cannakale.

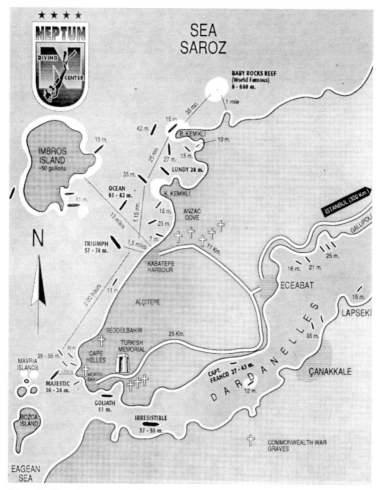

Map 3. Sketch map of shipwreck sites around the Gallipoli Peninsula.
(Neptune Diving Centre, Cannakale)

large ferry leaves and returns on the hour and it is prompt! As you cross the Narrows, you will see a Turkish memorial with words carved into the hillside above Kilitbahir which mean, *Traveller, halt! The soil you tread once witnessed the end of an era.* Another sign just above the town of Cannakale commemorates the important Turkish victory on 18 March 1915 against the Allied fleet. On arrival in Eceabat turn left, drive along the coast and follow the signs to Kilitbahir. You will pass the Gallipoli National Park Centre, some Turkish memorials and a Turkish grave, a military barracks, and drive through the small fishing village and ferry port of **Kilit Bahir** (2) 5 kms from Eceabat. The remains of Kilitbahir Fort are impressive. Begun in 1452, and extensively restored over the centuries, it is open to the public. In 1915

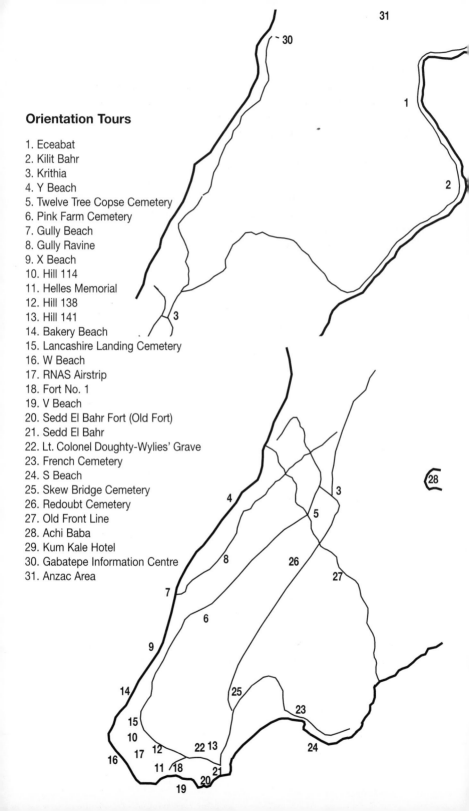

Orientation Tours

1. Eceabat
2. Kilit Bahr
3. Krithia
4. Y Beach
5. Twelve Tree Copse Cemetery
6. Pink Farm Cemetery
7. Gully Beach
8. Gully Ravine
9. X Beach
10. Hill 114
11. Helles Memorial
12. Hill 138
13. Hill 141
14. Bakery Beach
15. Lancashire Landing Cemetery
16. W Beach
17. RNAS Airstrip
18. Fort No. 1
19. V Beach
20. Sedd El Bahr Fort (Old Fort)
21. Sedd El Bahr
22. Lt. Colonel Doughty-Wylies' Grave
23. French Cemetery
24. S Beach
25. Skew Bridge Cemetery
26. Redoubt Cemetery
27. Old Front Line
28. Achi Baba
29. Kum Kale Hotel
30. Gabatepe Information Centre
31. Anzac Area

the fort held 19 guns.

As you continue along the Straits, it is hard to believe that in 1915 there were a minimum of 55 guns in eleven batteries, forming the Intermediate and Inner defences of the coast. You will notice several Turkish smaller fortifications, gun emplacements, ammunition bunkers, a statue of a Turkish soldier holding a massive shell and the Havuzlar Memorial and Cemetery, the site of four siege guns used to bombard the Allied ships. These all have significance as far as the Naval battle of 18 March 1915 is concerned but are not in the remit of this book.

After about ten kilometres, turn right and take the road which winds inland towards Krithia, passing vineyards, olive groves, the small village of Behramli and driving through some lovely scenery, with the hills and plateau of Kilit Bahr on your right, and rugged hills on your left. About 20 kms from Eceabat, you will approach a road junction with a sign to Gabatepe (Kabatepe) and the Anzac area. Do not turn right but continue to the village of Krithia (Alcitepe). Look left and you have a good view of the low hill of Achibaba, the objective for 25 April at Helles.

Krithia (3) is a natural stop. We suggest you visit one of the local cafes, have a cool drink and study the map. You will also return to Krithia at the end of your Helles tour. Your suggested route now is the anti-clockwise direction. In other words, as you enter Krithia from the north, turn right at the main cross roads and follow the Twelve Tree Copse sign. After a short distance, a fork in the road (3) is reached. Turning right here will take you in the direction of **Y Beach (4)**, which is, without question, the most difficult beach to find and details are included under the Walk No. 1 Y Beach section. The visit to Y Beach also will take at least 3 hours and could be a separate issue and therefore to avoid confusion, we suggest you continue on the orientation Tour bearing in mind that Y Beach is approximately at 3 o'clock.

Continue on the road signposted **Twelve Tree Copse CWGC Cemetery (5)**, which was made after the Armistice and will be found after about 1 km. You should be able to see the Helles Memorial in the far distance at about 12 o'clock, and the Turkish Memorial at 10 o'clock.

After about a further 3kms. **Pink Farm CWGC Cemetery (6)** will be seen on the left hand side of the road, where Brigadier-General Marshall, having landed at X Beach, eventually set up his Brigade HQ. In the small wood to the northeast of the cemetery can be seen remains of old trench lines, together with the foundations and a well belonging to the original Pink Farm.

Continuing along the route, after about 500 metres and having passed a lone tree on the bend on the right hand side, the rough grass track which leads down to **Gully Beach (7)** (known as Y2) and **Gully Ravine (8)** will be seen. This area eventually became the HQ for the 29th Division and was the scene of desperate fighting, particularly on 28th June 1915.

Continue along the road for about 1km. and on the right hand side, a small turning down a rough track to **X Beach (9)** will be found. This is easy to miss, so drive carefully. Looking straight ahead, and due south, the slope rises to **Hill 114 (10)**. The **Helles Memorial (11) and Hill 138 (12)** are at about 10 o'clock whilst further to the left **Hill 141 (13)** with the watertower on top, can also be clearly seen. Unknown to the planners at the time, it is also possible to see Morto Bay (S Beach). Continuing south, after about 500 m there is a small indentation in the cliff top. Below, on the right hand side, is **Bakery Beach (14)**. The road gradually bends round to the left and about 2kms from X Beach, **Lancashire Landing CWGC Cemetery (15)** will be seen on the right hand side. It is situated on Hill 114 and was begun immediately after the landing.

Continue for another 500 m until you come to a fork. To visit **W Beach (16)**, you will need to turn sharp right along a rough track until you reach a disused hut where you can park and then walk to the beach.

Gunners firing from postions at Helles.

To continue with this orientation tour, drive on towards the Helles memorial, passing the site of a small **RNAS airstrip (17)** on your right. You can turn right to the **Helles Memorial** where there is good parking. To continue, follow the signs to V Beach CWGC Cemetery. At the edge of what is a small amphitheatre, immediately on the right hand side before you descend the hill is **Fort No. 1(18)** with **V Beach (19)** just below. Drive on the rough track with V Beach on your right and you will pass the remains of **Sedd El Bahr Fort (Fort No.3) (20)** and enter the village of **Sedd El Bahr (21)**, the scene of grim house to house fighting on 26 April. Driving northwards, just before you leave the village, on the left hand side, is the road leading to Hill 141 and the **isolated grave of Lieutenant Colonel Doughty-Wylie (22)** However, we suggest you continue on the main road and after about 2 kms take the right fork signposted to Cannakale Sehitligi. This will take you to S Beach. As you now drive along the bay, you will note the **French**

23

National Cemetery and Memorial (23) on your left, set back off the road. You will arrive at **S Beach (24)** and, at its far end, you will see the Turkish Memorial and the site of De Tott's Battery. From here it is necessary to return on the same road and, at the main fork, turn right to continue towards Krithia and Eceabat. You will pass **Skew Bridge CWGC Cemetery (25)** on your right, formed after the Second Battle of Krithia in early May 1915.

You are now travelling in the direction the troops took in the ensuing battles and will pass positions on the right hand side, well known to the men of the Royal Naval Division, including Backhouse Post, whilst over the crest of Observation Hill will bring you near the sites of White House and Brown House. **Redoubt CWGC Cemetery (26)** will be found after about 3 kms from Skew Bridge on the left hand side of the road, and close by the infamous Vineyard, the scene of bitter fighting. Just 2 kms short of Krithia you pass through the **old Front Line (27)**, which was the furthest point the Allied troops reached in this area in 1915. On the right hand side in the far distance can be seen **Achi Baba** hill **(28)**, the main objective on the first day of the battle.

Having visited all the beaches, and arrived back in Krithia, it is suggested you drive back through the village and return to the junction marked Kabatepe, turn left and return to Eceabat by travelling north past the **Kum Kale Hotel** and camping complex **(29)** to a small junction. Turn right, pass the **Gabatepe Information Centre (30)** which houses a small museum, and travel east for about ten kms to Eceabat.

During this journey, the whole of the **battlefield area of the Australians and New Zealanders (31)** will be on your left hand side, with monuments marking such infamous places as **Lone Pine, Chanuk Bair and Scrubby Knoll** clearly seen. On arriving at the coast, turn right and proceed to **Eceabat** and the ferry port. You will pass a garage on your right – we know the owner is one of the most honest people on the Peninsula! It is essential to have a full tank of fuel before beginning a car tour, and there are now several petrol stations in Cannakale but with very few at Eceabat.

When you do stop at various places on this itinerary, make sure you safely park your vehicle well off the road and take any valuables with you. However, we would say that in all the years we have been visiting Gallipoli we have never had any problems with theft or vandalism, and have always found the Turkish people very kind, polite and extremely helpful and are sure that you will have a safe and memorable visit.

Chapter One

WHY DID IT HAPPEN? THE DARDANELLES UP TO 1915

At the south western end of the Black Sea is an outlet known as the Bosphorous and this runs for some 17 miles until it enters the small inland sea known as the Sea of Marmara. At this juncture is the Golden Horn inlet and the City of Istanbul, originally known as Constantinople.

The Sea of Marmara extends for some 105 miles down to Nagara Point, some 17 miles from the sea where, flowing southwest, it reduces into a long narrow channel. From a width of 2000 yards at Nagara Point it is further reduced after three miles to 1600 yards when it bends south westerly between the towns of Eceabat and Cannakale, at which point the channel is called the Narrows. From here it widens to four and a half miles at Erinkeui Bay and reduces to two miles by the time it enters the sea at Helles, the south western tip of the Gallipoli Peninsula. The average depth of the water is between 25 and 50 fathoms (150 feet to 300 feet) throughout its length. There is a permanent current of some 2-3 knots (three and a half miles per hour) down channel; with a strong south westerly gale against the run of the tide, severe conditions occur.

The Dardanelles is the name given to that long channel (some forty one miles) which connects the Sea of Marmara to the eastern Mediterranean and for that reason has always attracted attention for its strategic position.

There had been an earlier attempt to force the Dardanelles by the British Admiral Duckworth in 1807, when Britain assisted Russia against Turkey. This was a purely naval attempt, (despite there being a large number of British troops in the locality), and it failed, but the lessons were forgotten in 1915. The Royal Navy still thought it could take the channel without military assistance because, despite the fact that the shore batteries had been strengthened in the 1880s, the Royal Navy considered, quite rightly that, gun for gun, they, the Royal Navy, were superior. The main British warships had 12 inch guns whilst HMS *Queen Elizabeth* had 15 inch.

But the British ignored the German influence! The two men in Turkey at that time who were causing considerable trouble to the British were Talaat Bey and Enver Pasha, the latter to be appointed Minister of War in January

Enver Pasha Turkish Minister of War.

Marshal Liman von Sanders, the German GOC, Turkish Fifth Army.

1914, who were instrumental in eventually bringing Turkey into the First World War, alongside Germany.

One of their first acts was to invite 70 German officers on a military mission, who arrived in 1913. The head of the mission was one General Liman von Sanders who, in January 1914, was to be appointed Inspector General of the Turkish Army. Within months there was a vast improvement in that organization.

But if Turkey did have any reservations at that time on which side she should join, two events occurred which seemed to seal the decision.

1. On losing Lemnos, Imbros and Myteline to Greece during the Balkan Wars (1912) Turkey ordered two battleships from Great Britain. They raised the cost by public subscription, so one can imagine the outcry when on 3 August, 1915 Turkey, having already paid £3,000,000 sterling and with a Turkish crew waiting on Tyneside to board, found that the British had cancelled the contract and repossessed both ships. Thereafter they were known as HMS *Agincourt* and HMS *Erin* and they remained in British possession.

2. The second incident of note was the arrival in the Dardanelles of the German ships *Goeben* and *Breslau*.

On 15 August Admiral Limpus (he had been in charge of the naval guns at the Battle of Colenso in South Africa in 1899), whilst in command of the British Naval Mission in Turkey, was removed at the Turks' request. Also about that time Admiral Souchon was appointed C in C of the Turkish Navy, and from that moment both the Ottoman Army and Navy came effectively under German control.

In late October Admiral Souchon led the Turkish fleet into the Black Sea and shelled Odessa. On 30 October, the Russian, British and French Ambassadors demanded their passports, and the following day, 31 October 1914, Turkey declared war on the Entente.

It was Lord Fisher, the First Sea Lord, who sowed the seed of the thought that the Straits could be forced by a purely naval attack. Whilst Fisher had also stated that the assistance of Bulgaria and Greece would be beneficial to an attack on the Turks, it was understood that Greece would not march whilst Bulgaria's attitude remained uncertain and this would not change until Bulgaria saw a British military success in the region. This thinking was to influence the situation in Salonika later that year.

The Mediterranean theatre.

Discussions were now in hand with Admiral Carden, newly appointed to command the Dardanelles Squadron, and a plan was devised for forcing the Dardanelles without the assistance of troops, although it was acknowledged that it would be desirable for some ground forces to land and consolidate a naval success. However, Lord Kitchener stated categorically that a large number of troops were not available and so a purely naval attack was authorised.

The date of this attack was to be 19 February 1915 but, three days before this, a meeting of the War Council confirmed that some troops should be concentrated in the area in case their assistance be required.

So here is a clear instance of the politicians acknowledging the possible use of the Army. Another decision taken at that time was to despatch the 29th Division to Mudros, but its departure was delayed for some weeks due to pressure from the French who wanted it earmarked for France. In the meantime Kitchener decided that the Australian and New Zealand Corps, at that time training in Egypt, should be sent to the Dardanelles. On 20 February he sent a warning order to General Maxwell, commanding British troops in Egypt, for 36000 Anzac troops under Lieutenant General Sir WR Birdwood to stand by. All this coincided with the Admiralty sending the Royal Naval Division to Mudros to join two battalions of marines already there, arriving on 12 March.

Also at this time the French Government, which had already agreed to send a Naval Squadron to assist the British, resolved to despatch an army division to the Eastern Mediterranean. The latter was to be known as the *Corps D'Expeditionaire d'Orient* (CEO).

Total land troops now available in early March consisted of:

Royal Naval Division	10,000
Anzac corps	36,000
French troops	18,000
Total	64,000

Eventually permission was given for the 29th Division, under their General Officer Commanding, Major General Sir Aylmer Hunter-Weston, to leave for the Dardanelles on 10 March, adding an additional 18000 men.

Meanwhile Admiral Carden prepared a plan which was take the Gallipoli Peninsula and Constantinople and gave himself a time limit of three to four weeks to achieve this.

Winston Churchill, as First Lord of the Admiralty, continued to be very enthusiastic about the scheme.

Vice Admiral S Carden RN.

Winston Churchill, as First Lord of the Admiralty.

Major General Sir Aylmer Hunter-Weston

Turkish Situation

Whilst the Turkish air force and navy played a minor role in the forthcoming war, it was the army that was to become Turkey's strength.

As mentioned earlier it was the appointment of Liman von Sanders as Inspector General that greatly improved the situation. Subsequently, in March 1915, he was offered and accepted the post of Commander in Chief of the Turkish Fifth Army, with its headquarters in Gelibolu (Gallipoli town). Later as a Field Marshal he would be appointed supreme commander of the Turkish forces in Palestine in 1918 and lost a great battle against General Edmund Allenby in September of that year.

In August 1914 the main defence of the Dardanelles were the forts on both sides of the channel from Cannakale to the mouth at Helles. This was called the fortress by the Turks and consisted of three lines:

1. Outer defences: Four permanent forts at the toe of the Peninsula, two on either side, but which only provided four serviceable guns, each having a range of 16,000 yards. There were also field howitzers at Tekke Burnu.

Naval attack, 18 March 1915.

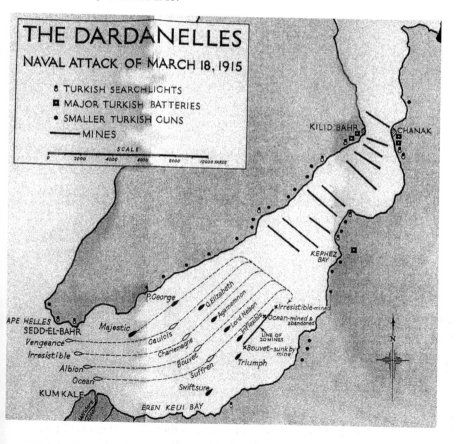

Kilid Bahr Fort – part of the inner defences.

2. Intermediate defences: At Kephez Point, some ten miles from the mouth of the Straits, were four works with a fifth on the opposite European shore. The principal fort of Dardanos had two 6 inch guns

3. Inner defences: These contained the heaviest guns in the Narrows.

There were five forts on the European shore and six on the Asiatic shore. Whilst all this meant that there were seventy two heavy and medium guns available, only a small number, including some 14 inch and 9.4 guns, were capable of long range fire (range between 15,000 and 17,000 yards).

The harbour at Gellibolu.

To summarise this aspect, out of a total of some one hundred heavy and medium guns *in situ* in 1914, only 14 were long range, there was a scarcity of ammunition and the crews were not well trained. There were also two searchlights, one at the entrance to the Straits and the other at the Narrows

During late 1914 and early 1915 the Turks improved their defences along the Dardanelles. Some 500 German officers and men were drafted in to reorganize the garrisons and the forts. The minefield was expanded and by November five lines of mines had been laid and four more searchlights put in place. By early 1915 the Turkish peacetime establishment had been increased from 36 Divisions to 45 Divisions (the Turkish establishment for a division included about 9000 rifles). In total over 70 divisions were raised, but many of these were used as reinforcement formations.

Action at last

The result of the considerations made by the British War Council were two major naval battles, both fought without any apparent assistance from the army

The first took place on 19 February 1915, with Admiral Carden as C in C and Rear Admiral de Robeck as second in command. The chief of staff was Commodore Roger Keyes. Admiral Carden's fleet consisted basically of old warships, namely HMS *Inflexible* (Flagship), HMS *Vengeance* (Rear Admiral de Roebeck) and three or four older battleships and light cruisers, together with four old French battleships.

The bonus was the newest and largest warship then in existence in the Royal Navy, HMS *Queen Elizabeth*. Her inclusion was a gamble by the Admiralty. Her keel was laid down at Portsmouth on 21 October

Captain G P W Hope of HMS *Queen Elizabeth*.

1912 and she was launched on 16 October 1913. She was the first ship in His Majesty's Navy to carry 15 inch guns and the first capital ship to be driven entirely by oil fuel. Captained by GPW Hope RN, she was indeed the pride of the Royal Navy and known to the men as the Queen Lizzie. She joined the Eastern Mediterranean Squadron, as it was called, off the entrance to the Dardanelles on 19 February, giving the fleet a total of 274 medium and heavy artillery pieces.

Also in the force were the two battalions of marines from the Royal Naval Division sent out by Churchill on the 6 February.

19 February was a wintry Mediterranean day, with excellent visibility and every detail of the forts could be seen quite clearly. The Fleet bombarded the forts, including the one at Kum Kale, but the attack was suspended later that day as the weather brought strong gales, which lasted some time. For a few days the Squadron anchored off Tenedos by day and cruised to the south by night. The 25 February was the next fine day, and the Squadron went back into the attack with a heavy bombardment on several of the forts in and around Cape Helles, in particular the Old Fort at the village of Sedd El Bahr (No. 3 Fort) and also No. 1 Fort, Cape Helles, which contained six big guns, including two modern 9.4 guns. Some remains can be seen there today, and it is interesting to note that two of them were put out of action on 25 February 1915 by Y turret of HMS *Queen Elizabeth* at a range of 12,100 yards. The British then realised that some of the guns in the Turkish defences were on retractable mountings, which made it extremely difficult for British gunners to get a direct hit.

On the 26 February both HMS *Vengeance* and HMS *Irresistible* landed demolition parties of marines, the former on the Asiatic coast near the Kum Kale pier and the latter on the European side at the Camber, east of Sedd El Bahr. It was then that Lieutenant Commander EG Robinson of HMS *Vengeance*, with the former party, won the Victoria Cross. He carried out the demolition of two guns on his own, refusing to be accompanied by the marines who were in their conspicuous uniforms. Two months later he would be promoted commander after destroying the stranded British submarine E15.

The party from HMS *Irresistible* were successful in destroying the remaining four guns in Fort No. 1 but failed to reach Tekke Burnu. It is salutary to note that these marines completed their mission at the Camber without suffering any casualties yet, some two months later, in the same vicinity, the 29th Division suffered 3,000 before nightfall.

Several raids were made in the ensuing days, including those on 4 March when detachments of marines from the Plymouth Battalion,

A modern submarine in the Narrows.

under their commanding officer, Lieutenant Colonel GE Matthews, landed and met severe opposition in the ruined villages of Sedd El Bahr and Yeni Kehr on the Asiatic coastline, south west of Kum Kale. They suffered over fifty casualties, and were withdrawn, but nevertheless their efforts contributed greatly to the fall of the outer forts.

And so this naval offensive came to a halt. There had no progress against either the inner or intermediate defences, or the minefields, but the outlying forts had been silenced. Perhaps it could be said that these successes distorted the judgement of the Allies regarding future action. Greece now wanted to send troops to the Peninsula, and even Bulgaria seemed impressed with the Allied progress.

Churchill still had faith in Admiral Carden and his estimate of reaching the Marmara in fourteen days must have appeared extremely attractive to the War Council. By now there was a great impasse on the Western Front and hundreds of young men were dying each day 'chewing barbed wire', as Churchill wrote.

So despite expert military advice, the War Council, eagerly devouring Carden's plan for a second naval attack in the Straits, accepted the principle.

The Secretary to the Committee for Imperial Defence, Colonel Sir Maurice Hankey RM noted:

The idea caught on at once. The whole atmosphere changed. Fatigue was forgotten. The War Council turned eagerly from the dreary vista of a slogging match on the Western Front to brighter prospects, as they seemed, in the Mediterranean. The Navy, in whom everyone had implicit confidence and whose opportunities had so far been few and far between, was to come into the front line. Even French with his tremendous preoccupations caught something of the general enthusiasm.

Meanwhile, having been given notice of impending military action by the first naval battle, Turkey, under excellent German supervision, was consolidating her defences.

So the die was finally cast. The Royal Navy would go it alone again but the timing would coincidentally run parallel to a large build up of ground troops because :

...if the War Council only pledged itself for the moment to naval action they were, in reality, committed to military action on a large scale in the event of the attempt to force the Dardanelles by the Fleet alone proving successful. (Dardanelles Commission)

But of course, in hindsight, they were also committed to military action if the naval attempt failed, as events clearly showed.

General Sir Ian Hamilton

Bearing in mind that the number of Allied troops on operations was now approaching 75,000, it was felt necessary to appoint a Senior Officer to command the Mediterranean Expeditionary Force (MEF), as it was to be called, and General Sir Ian Hamilton was chosen. He was a soldier who had proved his worth in many different theatres of war and was certainly a brave man, despite various criticisms which have been levelled at him over the years. He was commissioned into the Gordon Highlanders, the old 92nd, and made a name for himself initially in the First Boer War in the Battle of Majuba, South Africa, in 1881 where he acquitted himself well. He also served in Afghanistan, India and Egypt. At one time he was Inspector-General of the Imperial Forces. It has been said he was recommended for the Victoria Cross on two occasions.

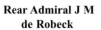

Rear Admiral J M de Robeck

General Hamilton and his new Chief of the General Staff, Major General Braithwaite, were transported rapidly to the Dardanelles in a matter of days, but unfortunately without a complete HQ and with very little practical information, such as detailed maps. They arrived just in time to view the second naval attack.

The following day Vice Admiral Carden hoisted his flag in *Queen Elizabeth* with Commodore Keyes as his Chief of Staff. However on 17 March the Vice Admiral was put on the sick list and replaced by Rear Admiral J M de Robeck. He confirmed to Winston Churchill that the plan for the forthcoming attack due to take place the following day was 'wise and practicable'.

For most of 18 March General Hamilton sailed in HMS *Phaeton*, looking at the coastline of the Peninsula, after which he wrote to Lord Kitchener:

> *Gallipoli looks a much tougher nut to crack than it did over the map in your office.*

At this time he decided to make the main base at Alexandria as Mudros lacked suitable docking facilities and sufficient fresh water, but the latter would serve as an excellent launching base for the landings.

To this day there is carved on the high cliffs in full view of the town of Cannakale, the date 18 March 1915, a constant reminder to the Turks and visitors alike of a day which started with such promise for the Allies but then ended in disaster.

At 10 am on the morning of 18 March, British and French ships, took up position off Cape Helles. The subsequent battle raged all day. In the early stages most of the guns in the forts were silent but the 12cm/15cm howitzer batteries were troublesome.

Initially matters went well for the Allies. A Turkish report states that at this time morale in their camp was low. An account quoted in the Official History by a Turkish General stated that by 2.00 pm the situation had become very critical:

> *All telephone wires were cut, all communication with the forts was interrupted, some of the guns had been knocked out, others were half buried, others again were out of action with their breech mechanism jammed; in consequence the artillery fire of the defence had slackened considerably.*

But as the French ship *Bouvet* turned to starboard to retire in Eren Keui Bay, she suffered a massive explosion and sank in two minutes, still

The French ship *Bouvet*.

steaming ahead. There were over 700 killed with only 48 survivors. It was later discovered that she had struck one of a new line of some eighteen mines which had been laid, unobserved, by the Turks, who had carefully noted the accustomed manoeuvre made by the British warships in earlier forays. The Turkish gunners, with renewed vigour, then returned to their guns and the course of the battle changed.

Both HMS *Irresistible* and HMS *Ocean* were sunk, whilst HMS *Inflexible*, *Souffren* and *Gaulois* were very badly damaged. That meant that one third of the Fleet, six capital ships, had became casualties and the fleet withdrew. The battle was over.

It was indeed a black day for the Royal and French navies and their failure ensured that the future conduct of the war in the Dardanelles would be a land campaign with naval support, despite the fact that some politicians still favoured another attempt by the Royal Navy alone.

On 22 March, at a conference on board HMS *Queen Elizabeth*, both General Hamilton and Admiral de Robeck agreed that it would be necessary to use the entire land force available to enable the Fleet to force the Dardanelles. The weather at that time was rough and unpredictable, but it was hoped that April would show some improvement.

Admiral de Robeck also informed the Admiralty that the Peninsula must be captured before he could take the Fleet into the Sea of Marmara with any degree of safety. The timing agreed by the two senior officers on board looked towards the middle of April for further action.

Churchill later told the Dardanelles Commission that both the Prime Minister and Mr. Balfour, with whom he had discussed the matter, were inclined to his view to insist on another naval attack. However, as the professional advisers and the Admiral on the spot were against it, it was impossible to go further, and he bowed to their decision.

Without question it has to be agreed that General Hamilton was faced with an enormous task. Whilst in no way is this account a judgement on his military abilities or his behaviour throughout this particular campaign, it must be remembered that he left London just a matter of days after his appointment, so little preparation or planning could have had been done before he arrived in the Dardanelles. They had many months to prepare for Normandy in June 1944!

The Allies were bereft of much intelligence or any detailed maps, despite the efforts of one Lieutenant Colonel Cunliffe Owen, later to serve on the Staff of the Anzac Corps, who had been Military Attaché in Constantinople in 1913. Then he had made a useful survey of the Dardanelles, including sites of batteries and minefields. Unfortunately this valuable work was ignored.

Security was appalling. It proved necessary to buy all the small craft available in Egypt, together with jerry cans and much of the thousand and one items one finds in the Quartermaster's Stores, as none had been supplied from UK; whilst news of the arrival and departure of transports and troops were freely mentioned in the Egyptian press, quite often giving details of army units, including their name and strength.

During this time the decision to set up the base in Alexandria by General Hamilton was amply and fully justified. In the hurry of embarkation in the UK the contents of the ships holds had been completely mixed and there was no alternative but to unload, sort and reload. One of the infantry battalions of the 29th Division had been embarked on four different vessels, units had been separated from their transport, wagons from their horses and guns from their ammunition, showing a complete lack of co-ordination in pre-planning. Ammunition was another problem. Rifle ammunition was scarce with an allocation of only about 500 rounds per rifle. The 29th Division had been issued with Mark 7 rifles whilst the RND had been given Mark 6 rifles, but whilst the Mark 7 rifles could use the Mark 6 ammunition, the Mark 6 rifles could not use the Mark 7 ammunition.

General Hamilton was then informed that a Russian Corps would be available in Odessa, to come under command of the British for the eventual attack on Constantinople, but could not play an active part in the landings. It was proved later that they did achieve the result of detaining three Turkish divisions in the Bosphorous until after the landings.

The strength of the Mediterranean Expeditionary in April was in the region of 80,000 troops, plus over 16,000 animals and 3,000 vehicles.

The preplanning for the landings had to be made quickly by the staff and in some detail. These included the marshalling of over a hundred ships and boats, the setting up of general hospitals and casualty evacuation and a detailed timetable for the landings. The alphabet was used to designate the transport ships, with each main force being designated a letter and then each ship numbered serially.

By the middle of April the entire Anzac Corps and the 29th Division were on Mudros whilst the large harbour:

was now so crowded with vessels of every imaginable

description, from the majestic Queen Elizabeth to the humble North Sea trawler, and from the proud Atlantic liner to the dirtiest of Thames tugs.

In fact it was so crowded that thirty four transports of the RND and the French troops had to wait at Trebuki Bay, on the island of Skyros, some eighty miles from Lemnos.

And everyone waited and waited!

The Grand Plan

It was about 23 March that General Hamilton and his staff produced an appreciation for the actual landings.

Taking all the factors into account, it was decided that the principal objective was the capture of the main Kilid Bahr plateau, a huge feature running some four miles west of the coastal village of Kilid Bahr and rising between 600 and 800 feet. It dominated the Inner Defences on both sides of the Straits and really was the key to the Dardanelles. Ownership of this strategic position would enable the army to carry out its primary task to assist the fleet to force the Dardanelles.

The plan also had to include the choice of landing beaches that would allow maximum assistance from the fleet. Ultimately it was agreed that the main thrust would come from three separate landings at the south of the peninsula, on beaches designated X -W -V with two lesser landings, one on each flank, on beaches Y and S, by troops of

The 'Helles Hand'. A Sketch by Lt Col J H Patteson. (Zion Mule Corps 1915)

Kilid Bahr village and port.

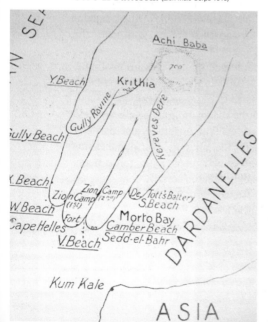

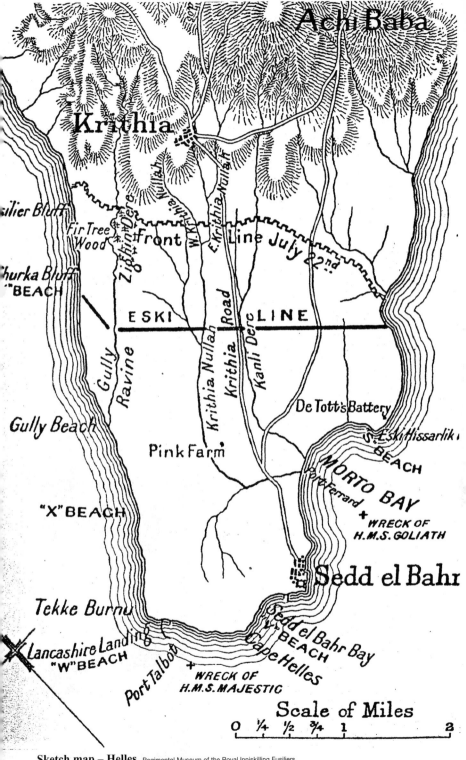

Achi Baba

Krithia

silier Bluff

Fir Tree
Wood

hurka Bluff
"BEACH

Front Line July 22nd

ESKI LINE

Gully Beach

Pink Farm

De Tott's Battery

S. Eski Hissarlik
BEACH

MORTO BAY

"X"BEACH

WRECK OF
H.M.S. GOLIATH

Sedd el Bahr

Tekke Burnu

Lancashire Landing
"W"BEACH

Port Talbot

Sedd el Bahr Bay
BEACH
Cape Helles

WRECK OF
H.M.S. MAJESTIC

Scale of Miles

0   ¼   ½   ¾   1   2

Sketch map – Helles. Regimental Museum of the Royal Inniskilling Fusiliers

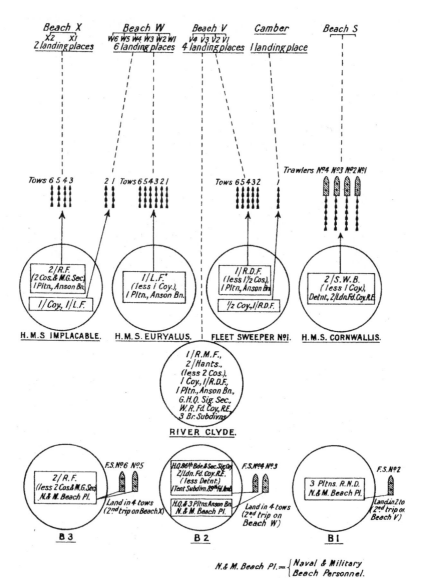

Diagram of the Helles landing.

the famous 29th Division. The beaches were named as the alphabet, but in reverse order. As the letter T might be mistaken for the letter V, it was omitted. The letter Z referred to the Anzac beach, which would be on the west coast of the peninsula around Gaba Tepe. On the Diagram of the Helles Landings, the number of landings places on each beach will be noted, with W Beach being the most complicated.

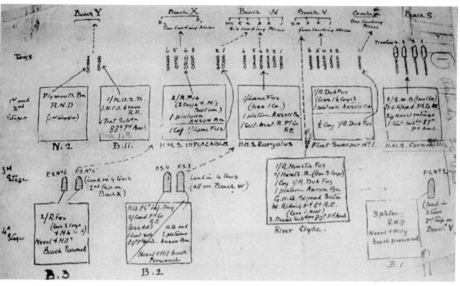

Original sketch plan for landings on 25 April.

In addition to the above there were to be three diversionary actions, one in the Gulf of Saros by the Royal Naval Division and two in the Kum Kale area by French troops.

The objective on the first day for the 29th Division was the small but imposing Achi Baba hill, over 750 feet high. Although not giving a view of the defences of the Narrows, it certainly overlooked the exits of the designated landing beaches and would be an excellent jumping off point to attack the Kilid Bahr plateau.

Turkish Forces

During the activity of the Allies over the past few months the Turks had been gradually building their defences and by late April Liman Von Sanders had at his disposal six divisions divided into three units i.e.

1st Combat Group: 5th and 7th Divisions at Bulair

2nd Combat Group: 9th Division in the south

3rd Combat Group: 3rd and 11th Division at Kum Kale/Besika Bay

In reserve: 19th Division

(A total establishment of some 54,000 men)

HQ Fifth Army : Gellibolu

This narrative is concerned only with the 9th Division (26th Regiment).

Eventually, the date of the landings was set as 23 April, subsequently amended twice due to inclement weather conditions, firstly to 24 April and finally to 25 April. The timings of the landings would vary slightly between beaches, but basically would be about thirty minutes after daybreak to enable the crews to see the landing beaches.

The Order of Battle: 29th Division
VIII Corps Commander – Lieutenant General Hunter-Weston

86 Brigade	**87 Brigade**
1/Royal Fusiliers	1/Royal Inniskilling Fusiliers
1/Lancashire Fusiliers	2/South Wales Borderers
1/Royal Munster Fusiliers	1/Border Regiment
1/Royal Dublin Fusiliers	1/King's Own Scottish Borderers

88 Brigade
2/Worcestershire Regiment
2/Hampshire Regiment
1/Essex Regiment
1/5 Royal Scots

In addition to the above, a number of Royal Engineers were to land at X W and V Beaches and prepare to work on piers and jetties.

29th Division Memorial, Stretton on Dunsmore, Warwickshire, rededicated on 23 September 2001.

HMS *Queen Elizabeth* hosted Sir Ian Hamilton and his staff , who boarded her on 24 April. Two members of the staff that day were Major Aspinall, who was to write the Official History of the Gallipoli Campaign, and Major John Churchill, brother of Winston Churchill.

On 25 April, the *Queen Lizzie* oversaw the landings of the Anzac Corps at Ari Burnu and later the 29th Division at Helles. On 14 May HMS *Queen Elizabeth* left Mudros Harbour to rejoin the grand Fleet at Scapa Flow. It was the end of her involvement in the Gallipoli Campaign, but it does seem fitting that it was in her Admiral's dining room, three and a half years later, that Admiral Beatty received the surrender of the German Grand fleet.

So now the scene was set for what to become one of the most tragic and controversial campaigns of the First World War.

42

Chapter Two

Y BEACH – WHAT MIGHT HAVE BEEN

In General Sir Blumberg's *A Record of the Royal Marines During the War 1914-1918* entitled *Britain's Sea Soldier*, he refers to 25 April as, 'the day of the Great Adventure'.

It was indeed an adventure for not just the Plymouth Battalion and the Royal Marine Light Infantry detachment of HMS *Cornwallis* (the only Royal Marine units actually landed that day, under Lieutenant Colonel Godfrey Matthews), but also for 1/King's Own Scottish Borderers under Lieutenant Colonel A S Koe and A Company 2/South Wales Borderers under Captain R G Palmer. The last were attached to Y force as there was lack of space on HMS *Cornwallis*, which was transporting the main body of 2/SWB to S beach.

Y Beach was about 6,000 yards from X Beach and some 3000 yards south west of Krithia, and the nearest beach to the main objective that day - the capture of Achi Baba. It consisted of a narrow strip of sand at the foot of steep, crumbling and forbidding cliffs, about 150 - 200 feet high, which were covered with thorny scrub. A steep gully ran from the beach to the cliff top as well as a number of smaller parallel gullies, which would have assisted the troops when climbing. The Turkish defenders appeared to have considered that these cliffs would deter any assault, so that they had not bothered to build any defences in the area.

Winston Churchill's brother Major Jack Churchill, a staff officer in the Dardanelles, wrote a few sardonic lines during the last stages of the campaign on the Peninsula which perhaps sums up the feeling of some of those who had to climb these cliffs.

> Y Beach, the Scottish Borderer cried,
> While panting up the steep hillside,
> Y Beach!
> To call this thing a beach is stiff,
> It's nothing but a bloody cliff.
> Why beach?

The Plan

The decision to land over 2,000 men here in the rear of the Turkish positions was taken quite late in the general planning. It had the main purpose of advancing inland, drawing Turkish forces and minimising

Trench Map – Helles (January 1916).

enemy reinforcements being sent to the south. A landing here would also assist in guarding the left flank of the proposed advance north.

The landing would take place at the same time as the bombardment started at Helles and Sedd El Bahr, with Y Force advancing inland. In addition they were to capture a Turkish gun reported to be in the area. It was later discovered that this gun did not exist. The men at Y Beach would then link up with the 29th Division when the latter conducted its proposed general advance over the Peninsula towards the Achi Baba ridge.

As will be seen, vague orders, difficulties of communication, misunderstandings and disagreement between the two battalion commanding officers; and the fact that it was discovered that the ammunition provided was incompatible with the rifles in the men's possession, caused Y Beach to pose its own special set of problems.

Control of the landings at X, W and V Beach was with GOC 86 Brigade, Brigadier General Hare, acting as covering force commander, and who was to land personally at W beach. Because of the distance, Y and S Beaches would be under direct control of the 29th Division HQ set up on the Flagship, HMS *Euryalus*.

In view of what was to occur that day, it would appear that the orders to Y Force were unclear. The command structure, too, was to prove confusing. There were two lieutenant colonels ostensibly in charge. At a Divisional conference Lieutenant Colonel Matthews CB, Royal Marines, was found to be the senior of the two and he was informed that this was so. However, Lieutenant Colonel Koe was too ill to attend this Conference, and for some time after the landing he believed himself to be in command. GHQ also thought that Colonel Koe was in command. It did not augur well, and did nothing to lessen the difficulties.

Lt Col A Koe, 1/KOSB.

Lieutenant Colonel G E Matthews, CB CMG RMLI. (Pictured later as a Brigadier General).

Verbal orders were given to Lieutenant Colonel Matthews, for example, to 'make contact' with X Beach, but he was uncertain whether this meant actual contact or just visual. In the event, neither were obtained. Another eventuality for which contingency plans were apparently not laid or orders given was the course of action to be taken by Lieutenant Colonel Matthews if the advance from the south did not materialise.

The landing

On the evening of 24 April, elements of Y force, transferring to the cruisers HMS *Amethyst* and HMS *Sapphire* and Transport N2, carrying Plymouth Battalion Royal Marine Light Infantry, left Mudros for a rendezvous four miles west of Y Beach, where they gathered at about 2.30 am on the morning of the 25 April.

All were transferred to the trawlers, and the whole flotilla steamed towards the shore. HMS *Goliath* stood off the beach about 4,000 yards away, with the cruisers further in at about 2,000 yards. At 4.15 am the trawlers and small boats started to steam boldly in under the cliffs. 1/KOSB were the first to land. Major (later Lt. Colonel) A J Welch noted:

> *About 2.30 am the battalion transhipped again... The night was calm but it was dark, and some of us wondered how a task of such nicety was to be executed. ...at 4.45 am on Sunday 25 April we hit the shore. Visibility had by then reached 100 yards, and there was every trawler in its exact position.*[1]

Lieutenant Stirling-Cookson wrote on 11 May 1915:

> *As soon as the trawlers pulled up we all got into the boats, rowed ashore, and jumped on to the beach.*

Private John Vickers, Plymouth Battalion RMLI, wrote more fully:

> *Preparing to land. Fell in with Field Dressing and Identity Discs. Prepared our marching order (which is rather weighty). It contains greatcoat, three pairs of socks, canteen and cover, towel and soap, flannel, hard brush, holdall containing knife, fork, spoon, comb, razor and brush, three days iron rations consisting*

Y Beach and its difficult approach.

DENSE
SCRUB

Y BEACH
LOOKING
SOUTH

of 2lb 'bully' beef and 2lb biscuits, a waterproof sheet weighing about 5lbs. We were to carry 250 rounds of ammunition weighing about 10lbs, a full waterbottle, rifle and bayonet. This completed our equipment and we could take what private property we wished...

As we drew near the land it grew light quite suddenly and we were able to see the point at which we were to land. It appeared from a distance to be an impossible landing, but as we drew nearer it was not so sheer as at first supposed..

The next few minutes were the most exciting I had experienced...We got out of the trawlers into small boats holding about 30 men and went inland. The boats grounded some 50 yards from shore and we jumped into the water and waded ashore – a very difficult task as the water was over our waists and we had a decent weight to carry[2]

They found the landing had been a complete surprise. Not a shot was fired from the shore. The men began to disembark without mishap and without being fired on by the enemy. Sir Ian Hamilton had decided that Gully Beach, a tempting cove some 1,000 yards to the south in the direction of X Beach, should be avoided as it would probably be well defended. In fact it is now known that there were just two platoons of the enemy at the mouth of Gully Ravine, with a further platoon at Sari Tepe; but still sufficient, of course, to effect serious damage on the attackers. In the dim light of dawn they men looked up at cliffs which seemed to tower above them.

The so called beach was a bouldery, pot holey foreshore, and many men landed far wetter than they expected. From the narrow strip of foreshore the cliff rose steeply, but not unclimbable, to a height of about 150 feet. Running NW from the beach was a steep stony nullah (a dry or wet water channel) which gave the best approach to the top. On the north side of the top of the nullah was a distinct bluff, higher than the surrounding ground. It commanded a fair field of fire. In fact, the site would have made an admirable base for further operations had it not been for the unexpected and unwelcome natural feature, afterwards known as Gully Ravine.[3]

Scouts were almost immediately able to confirm that there was no sign of the Turkish army, although four Turks were encountered; two were killed and two taken prisoner.

By 5.45 am, just one and a half hours later, it was reported that all troops were ashore safely, without meeting any opposition. The troops could hear the salvoes of HMS *Implacable* firing less than three miles away off X Beach, their nearest neighbours.

1/KOSB were capably supervised off the beach by the Military Landing Officer, Major McAlester, together with his able assistant Captain Ogilvy, but whilst the men had their packs, none had spades or picks. A considerable amount of hard work was required to drag ammunition, food and, most importantly, water to the top of the cliff. As a contrast to what was happening on W and V Beaches, the only casualties at this time on Y Beach were two men killed by a naval 'short'.

Sir Ian Hamilton passed Y Beach in HMS *Queen Elizabeth* at about 8.30 am on his way to Helles from Anzac. Hundreds of troops could be seen at that time sitting on the edge of the cliff, with working parties struggling up the steep path from the beach carrying water.

The KOSB War Diary noted that

> at 9.00 am part of 1/King's Own Scottish Borderers, the South Wales Borderers and the Royal Marine Light Infantry occupied a ridge in front, from where they could see the enemy but could not get in touch with them.

It was at about this time that the Commander in Chief, General Sir Ian Hamilton, felt that as the troops on V Beach seemed to be held up, reinforcements should be sent to Y Beach but, as General Hunter-Weston, although a subordinate, was in command of such reinforcements, he, Hamilton, could only suggest a change of plan. He had to signal twice to General Hunter-Weston before receiving half an hour later an emphatic 'no'. It should be pointed out that General Hunter-Weston was at that time off W Beach and unaware of the seriousness of the situation at V Beach. He was more concerned about reinforcing 1/Lancashire Fusiliers on W Beach.

Y Force had meanwhile taken up a defensive position on top of the cliff to protect the landing beach. It was so quiet that Lieutenant Colonel Matthews and his Adjutant walked across the top of Gully Ravine to within 500 yards of Krithia (Alci Tepe) completely unopposed. They saw no signs of the enemy and the village appeared deserted, probably because the two Turkish companies in reserve close by had been sent south when the main landings occurred.

It became a lovely spring day, and the countryside around Y Beach basked in warm sunshine. Patrols were sent out and Major Welch of 1/KOSB found the enemy entrenched in strength some 1,200 yards north of Y Beach but that they 'showed no aggressive spirit', although they barred the way of any further advance. His colleague Captain

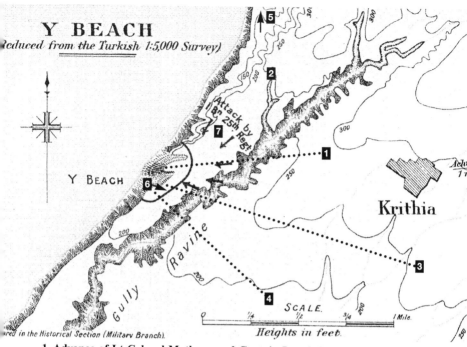

Y BEACH
Reduced from the Turkish 1:5,000 Survey)

Attack by Bn 25th Regt

Y BEACH

Krithia

Ravine

Gully

SCALE.

0   ¼   ½   ¾   1 Mile.

Heights in feet.

red in the Historical Section (Military Branch).

1. Advance of Lt Colonel Mathews and Captain Lough 2. Turkish troops entrenched 3. Captain Cooper 4. Patrols sent out 5. Sari Tepe 6. British defensive zone 7. Turkish attack

Cooper went straight inland and saw Morto Bay quite clearly, together with the battleships firing off Sedd El Bahr, but encountered no enemy.

Two companies of marines reconnoitred for about a mile south east of the beach in search of the non-existent Turkish gun, completely undisturbed. That morning everything was very peaceful, in fact the men were to be unmolested for almost eleven hours, as the Turkish 1/26 Regiment, lying between Seme Tepe and Sari Tepe, just two miles north of Y Beach, were not utilised, being kept back to protect their

Krithia (Alcitepe) village today.

own area. But at about 11.30 am the Turks fired some artillery shots and troop movements were seen.

At this time Lieutenant Colonel Koe sent a message to X Beach:

> *OC KOSB to 86 Bde X Beach. 11.45 am KOSB are established at Y. (Marines) have advanced to 200 ridge. Have stored SAA on top of cliff. Shall I guard it and join you, or remain where I am? Have withdrawn* [sic] *from 200 ridge, as your advance would prevent my remaining there.*

It is clear from this message, which was ignored, that Lieutenant Colonel Koe believed he was in command at Y Beach. But despite its initial success, the landing at Y beach was not to be exploited.

By about 3.00 pm, when it became apparent that the anticipated advance from the south had not materialised, with no news of what was happening at the main landing beaches and as no fresh orders had been received, Colonel Matthews decided he must safeguard Y Beach.

Orders were given to bring back the advanced guards to a defensive zone formed on top of the cliff covering Y Beach, and await in particular the expected advance of 86 Brigade from the south.

An extract from the War Diary of A Coy 2/SWB briefly states:

> *Y Beach 25 April*
>
> *A Company under Captain RG Palmer in conjunction with the KOSBs and the RMLI effected a landing from HMS* Sapphire *and* Amethyst *at about 5am. The whole force was commanded by Colonel Matthews RMLI. No opposition was encountered and an advance was made to a line overlooking the Krithia - Sedd El Bahr Road in order to flank any Turkish retirement. By noon, as no communication could be obtained between the force and Divisional Headquarters, the former retired to a line semi circular to the landing place...*

The troops had toiled and sweated, digging an extended line, without proper equipment in the very hard dry soil, for the most part only eighteen inches deep with many roots. The men were thinly deployed - the three companies of the Plymouth Battalion on the right, A Company 2/ SWB next to them, then 1/KOSB and finally the fourth company of the Plymouth Battalion near the cliff edge. In other words, the regular troops were in the middle.

> *The line was formed by the men's packs and with entrenching tools. It never reached what could be called a trench, and was constructed under a most harassing and ever increasing rifle fire.*[4]

Although never a serious menace, bursts of artillery and sniping caused some aggravation during the construction of the frail fort. However hostilities began in earnest at about 4.00 pm when a Turkish battalion arrived in the Y Beach area from Serafin Farm, near Kilid Bahr, where Colonel Sami Bey commanded the Turkish 9th Division. A series of spasmodic attacks were begun against the British left from the Turkish trenches. These persisted until dusk (about 7.00 pm) when the Turks retired behind a ridge 900 yards from the British left flank, but at 7.30 pm a further fierce attack was renewed with incessant firing, this time all along the line from Gully Ravine. Shouts and bugle calls from the enemy lines could be clearly heard. These determined attacks resulted in a critical situation, with the danger that the force could have been split into two, and the line breached in several places. Hand to hand fighting took place and a desperate struggle ranged in the rain and darkness. At about 11.00pm two Turkish companies arrived from Serafin Farm, making a total of some 1800 men.

The Turks were determined 'to drive the English into the sea' and hurled themselves grimly at their enemy, and with the use of bayonets, bombs and machine guns did their utmost to achieve their purpose. Some Turks managed to get between the thin khaki line and the cliff top, including a machine gun party, but these were peremptorily dealt with.

The enemy made four main attacks, evidently probing the British defensive line for weak spots. At times they were within ten yards of their shallow trenches and in some places actually reached them. On one occasion, it is recorded, a German officer walked up to the 1/King's Own Scottish Borderers section of the trench and demanded their surrender. He was summarily dismissed by being hit on the head with a spade by a man who was improving his trench.

During the night Lieutenant Colonel Matthews signalled desperately for reinforcements on two occasions but received no reply - indeed neither message was even acknowledged. Sergeant Will Meatyard, HQ Coy, Plymouth Battalion Royal Marine Light Infantry, wrote:

I had received orders to take no signal lamps whatever when we landed but when night came we found that a signal lamp was badly needed, there being no other means of communication. By a stroke of luck I thought of the COs torchlight pocket lamp, and with this I was able to send quite a number of important signals. My fingers got rather sore working the small slide up and down...

In this age of satellites, mobile telephones and text messages, it is hard to imagine that such a basic method of communication had to be relied upon.

At about 5.30am on 26 April, by request of Lieutenant Colonel Matthews, some 30,000 rounds of ammunition were sent ashore by steam boat from HMS *Sapphire*,

Major Welch OC A Company, 1/KOSB, noted:

> *Just before dawn the Turks eased their attacks, but not for long. At 6 am they launched a massed attack against the whole line, pouring in waves out of the great gully. At that very moment one of our guardian angels, HMS Goliath, for once sent a short shell. It fell in the middle of our line.*

This could have done nothing to lessen the tension and strain after such a stressful night. Although one could hardly have blamed 1/KOSB if they had wavered and made for the beach, the Regimental History proudly declares:

> *But they did not. They rallied and returned to the old line with a cheer, led by their Colonel Koe, a sick man and a hero. He received his death wound, but he saved the situation.*

The troops at Y Beach had fought stubbornly and had suffered heavy casualties. They were exhausted and many had used up all their ammunition. Sir Ian Hamilton wrote warmly in his dispatch that the

> *British repeatedly counter charged with the bayonet and always drove off the enemy for the moment, but the Turks were in vast superiority.*

There was little hope of resisting another strong attack unless reinforcements and more ammunition arrived. But it appears that Lieutenant Colonel Matthews had no thought of evacuating his position, despite his anxiety and the seriousness of the situation.

It was perhaps unfortunate that no orders for a general attack were given, and hence no real advance could be made, as it became clear later that the total number of Allied troops at Y and S Beaches were greater than the number of Turks south of Achi Baba.

A Turkish officer directs a machine-gun crew overlooking the landing beaches.

Considerable conjecture and discussion has taken place regarding the events that occurred at Y Beach on 26 April, and many varied opinions have been aired. It was the one of the subjects under serious investigation during the enquiry by the subsequent Dardanelles Commission, which sat after the campaign had failed.

A series of alarmist messages had been received by the Navy from the beach during the early morning which hinted at 'real trouble ashore'. The supporting ships, which had lain offshore throughout 25 April ready to assist if required, had spent a frustrating day. Through no fault of their own, they were in complete ignorance of the position of the men ashore and were hampered in their wish to give assistance. They could not see the surrounding countryside as the edge of the cliff was too high.

Signal logs of the various support ships record such questions as 'Are any of our troops dressed in blue?' To the question 'Have you any idea of how things have been going?' posed despairingly from HMS *Amethyst*, the reply came back from HMS *Sapphire*, 'No news at all!'

The Navy then received a plea for help and sent off a number of small boats. It transpired that the call was made by a young officer who was over 500 yards to the south of the main beach and it was to the young man that the small boats were directed. They arrived there and took off some wounded.

The Official History notes:

> *The sight of troops re-embarking gave the impression to many of those at the main landing place that a withdrawal had begun; and when boats arrived at the beach to fetch the wounded, a number of unwounded stragglers also climbed in. Thus, all unknown to Colonel Matthews, and to the troops still holding the top of the cliff, the evacuation began.*

One can understand, perhaps, that in the terrifying uncertainty of what was expected of them and the state of complete exhaustion and strain after a night of ceaseless fighting, some unwounded men slithered down the steep path to the beach. It must also be remembered that some, too, were extremely young, had had little training, were inexperienced and out of touch with their units. This was true in particular of the Plymouth Battalion, which consisted of 75% recruits, 20% reservists and only 5% regulars.

Another violent attack took place by the Turks at about 7.00 am, which succeeded in breaking part of the British line in the centre and right, and some men were forced to retire down the cliff. It looked as if the weak line would break, as there were no reserves available, but a counter attack was organised. A Company SWB, led from the front by Captain Habershon, charged with bayonets and the situation was restored.

His action was most effective, the Turks broke and fled and
made no further attempt to attack.[5]

By 7.30 am 26 April it was all over. An uncanny calm suddenly fell, to
the great relief of everyone. The Turks, one and half battalions strong,
had withdrawn, but despite their lack of numbers, they had inflicted
heavy casualties on the invaders.

Lieutenant Colonel Matthews was seen pacing up and down on the
top of the cliff with his Adjutant, Captain Lough, until he discovered
that the trenches on his right flank were empty. He sent the following
signal to 29th Division:

7.45 am Situation critical. Urgent need reinforcements and
ammunition, without which cannot maintain ridge at Y.
Alternative is to retire on to beach under cover ships' guns.

He then gathered together all the men he could find and took up a
position at the head of the steep path leading to the beach, to cover the
removal of his wounded. By now he was aware of the fact that
unauthorised re-embarkation was taking place, but decided to allow it
to continue.

Sir Ian Hamilton became aware that the evacuation was in full
swing when he proceeded to Y Beach from Anzac at about 9.30 am on
26 April. When HMS *Queen Elizabeth* reached Helles with the
Commander in Chief on board, he was staggered to learn that General
Hunter-Weston was completely unaware that re-embarkation had even
begun. An urgent message was sent to HMS *Dublin* at 10.50 am
requesting a situation report. At 11.15 the following reply was
received:

Nearly all wounded embarked. Last ridge being held by
rearguard. Remainder of troops embarking.

Indeed by about 11.00 am all the men on the beach, wounded and
unwounded, had been embarked. No reply to Lieutenant Colonel
Matthew's desperate messages had been received from the 29th
Divisional HQ. There appeared to be no prospect of reinforcements. In
view of the complete lack of interest and support from the Division,
Lieutenant Colonel Matthews decided to withdraw his rearguard from
the top of the cliff. It was now too late to reverse the re-embarkation
and the only other course of action would have been a completely new
landing under fire.

So Y Beach was abandoned and yet, during the whole of the re-
embarkation, there had been no reaction from the enemy because
unknown to the British they themselves had been completely
withdrawn. It was not until over two months later that men of the 29th

Division again stood on the top of the cliff at Y Beach, the whole area eventually secured after the Battle of Gully Ravine (28 June - 5 July) with heavy fighting and loss of life. The Beach became an evacuation point for the medical services from the British front line, which was close by, and a forward supply position.

One can only have sympathy with Lieutenant Colonel Matthews, who, at the Dardanelles Commission enquiry, accepted full responsibility for the withdrawal. During the entire 29 hours he had held his position he had heard nothing from Divisional Headquarters. It could be said that perhaps he should have showed more initiative.

However, no Divisional Staff Officer was personally sent to assess the situation, not an impossible task as Headquarters was only twenty minutes away by boat. No one had even kept him informed of what was happening at the southern end of the Peninsula. It appeared to him he had been completely forgotten and ignored.

In his defence, it has to be said that Lieutenant General Hunter-Weston would have been very pre-occupied and anxious about the difficulties in front of him at Helles and Sedd El Bahr as the night wore on. Y Beach seemed a long way away and did not give him serious cause for concern until about 7.00 am on 26 April, when he passed on the request for help from Lieutenant Colonel Mathews onto GHQ stating that he himself had no reinforcements to spare. The Turks still held Sedd el Bahr and the hill behind it, and the landing at V Beach still had to be secured. So despite Lieutenant Colonel Matthews' constant appeals for assistance, Hunter Weston had decided on his priorities. The only action he took as a result of these messages was to warn X Beach to ensure their left flank was established firmly. He did not reply to Lieutenant Colonel Matthews, who seemed to have been left stranded between his Divisional Commander and GHQ.

The total British casualties suffered at Y Beach amounted to 697 - great loss for no gain. 1/KOSB alone had lost 296 Officers NCOs and men, including its Commanding Officer, Colonel Koe, who was severely wounded and taken off the beach, only to die of wounds 26 April. He was buried at sea and is commemorated on the Helles Memorial to the Missing.

Extracts from *The KOSB in the Great War* indicates the gallant spirit and bravery of some of those who took part:

Lieutenant Cheatle stood with bleeding head cheering on the men until he was killed.

Captain Antrobus shook hands with his comrades, and led them in the final recapture of the line, to fall when he reached it.

Group of officers, 1/KOSB, Lucknow, India, 1914.

Captain Marrow, Adjutant – shot in the head whilst speaking to Major McAlester the Commanding Officer. His head was shattered, and he fell dead over the Commanding Officer.

Major McAlester was awarded the DSO and later MID twice. He died in June 1928 and is buried in Ayr Cemetery, Ayr, Scotland.

The History refers to Captain Marrow as being irreplaceable, knowing his work well and being respected and adored by all ranks. To his fellow officers he was a prince of good fellows:

Lieutenant Commander Adrian Keyes wrote of the skill with which he (Captain Marrow) *had organized and directed the boat practice and the supply of food and ammunition from the beach to the front. During the black chaos of that awful night he seemed to be ubiquitous and always in the right place. Thanks to the daring and determination of his comrade and admirer, RSM Douglass, his body was found on the 'return journey' and he eventually was buried by Padre Reid beside his friend Captain Antrobus.*

Captain Marrow, Captain Antrobus and Lieutenant Cheatle now lie in Twelve Tree Copse British Military Cemetery, the nearest to Y Beach.

The RMLI Plymouth Battalion casualties amounted to 14 Officers and 317 NCOs and men. A biographical note in the 1917 edition of *Globe and Laurel* says that Brigadier General Godfrey Estcourt Matthews CB CMG joined the Royal Marines in 1884 when he was eighteen years old and served in Egypt and Sudan, being present at the battle of Omdurman. He was praised for his energy and devotion to duty.

Grave of Major McAlester DSO Ayr Cemetery. He was severely wounded at Gallipoli on 28 April 1915, after assuming command following the death of Lt Col Koe.

When serving as Officer Commanding the Khartoum District he earned the nickname *Abu Nadara* (Father of Glasses) as he wore a monocle. In the early days of the First World War he commanded a Royal Marine Battalion in Antwerp. After the Gallipoli campaign he served on the Western Front. He was mortally wounded on 12 April 1917 and died of his wounds the following day whilst GOC 198 Infantry Brigade RMLI

While visiting a battalion in the trenches he was wounded, and his Brigade Major killed, by a 5.9" shell. He was taken to the – Casualty Clearing Station in the town of –, where, early on the 13th, the biggest specialist who could be got operated on him. The injuries, which were very severe, were to the head. He never regained consciousness, and passed away at 5.30 pm the same day. He was buried at 3 pm on the 14th in the English portion of the - Town Cemetery..By a curious coincidence Matthews' old Band (Chatham Division RMLI) now on a tour in France, were in the town. They attended and played his remains to the cemetery. The bugles and firing party were provided by his own Brigade. ..His loss is very keenly and very genuinely felt in his Division. He was one of the best soldiers in the Corps, and one of the bravest men who ever wore uniform.

Brigadier General Mathews is buried in Bethune Town Cemetery, France.

A Company 2/SWB's casualties amounted to 70, including Captain Palmer, who is now commemorated on the Helles Memorial to the Missing. Born in Sydney, Australia he was educated in Scotland and Sandhurst and served in the South African War (MID) and with 2/South Wales Borderers in Tientsin between 1912/1914.

Lieutenant Guy Nightingale, 1/RMF, who had experienced more than his fair share of the horrors of the landing at V Beach, having seen, amongst many others, Brigadier General Napier, Major Jarret and Lieutenant Colonel Doughty Wylie die, found himself in early May in an old entrenchment above Y Beach. He shared it with the bodies of men from the King's Own Scottish Borderers who had been killed on the day of the landing. In *Irish Voices from the Great War* Miles Dungan quotes from a letter written by Nightingale at that time:

These bodies were still lying there highly decomposed and the stench was awful. In the dark we kept tumbling over the bodies and treading on them. When it was light I found I had dug in next to the remains of an officer in the KOSBs whom I had last seen at the Opera at Malta and had spent a most jolly evening with. There were ten KOSBs and seven South Wales Borderers lying there, but I only recognised a few.

It could all have been so different. Some military historians consider that a bold advance from Y Beach in the direction of S Beach on the morning of 25 April could have assisted in securing the south of the Peninsula.

Y Beach is in its way the most tragic incident in all the landings at Gallipoli. A far more promising opening than that secured at S Beach, its adequate exploitation might have made an incalculable difference. [6]

Deplorable as the heavy losses had been, and unfortunate as was the tactical failure to make good so much ground at the outset, yet, taking the operation as it stood, there can be no doubt it has contributed greatly to the success of the main attack, seeing that the plucky stand made at Y Beach had detained heavy columns of the enemy from arriving at the southern end of the peninsula during what it will be seen was a very tough-and-go struggle. [7]

Cleverly conceived, happily opened, hesitatingly conducted, miserably ended – such is the story of the landing at Y Beach...But the real value of Y Beach was appreciated by no one till the opportunity had passed. Compared with the advantages which must have accrued from a clearer grasp of the immense potentialities of this position on the enemy's flank, the results of the enterprise were heartbreaking.[8]

By 27 April 1/KOSB had been transferred from warships to HMT *Ansonia* and remained there throughout that day, during which a Memorial Service was arranged for their comrades.

2/SWB was now reunited with the remainder of their Battalion, who had landed at S Beach.

Plymouth Battalion RMLI transferred from HMS *Goliath* at 1.00 am on 27 April to their own transport. A Memorial Service was held for those had been left on the field of battle. The mournful strains of the bagpipes was heard playing the lament. At 6.00 am the Battalion landed at W Beach, where it was used for working parties.

1. The KOSB in the Great War – Captain Stair Gillon
2. From Trench and Turret – S M Holloway
3. & 4. The KOSB in the Great War – Captain Stair Gillon
5.& 6. The History of the South Wales Borderers – C T Atkinson
7. Despatch – 20 May 1915 Sir Ian Hamilton
8. Official History of the War – Military Operations Gallipoli Vol I

WALK NO 1 Y BEACH

The first obvious difference to following walking tours on, for example, the Somme or in the Ypres Salient is the distinct absence of useful trench maps for this particular period, which is of course understandable. Use has therefore been made of other sources, including contemporary sketches and Official History maps.

Starting Point: Krithia (Alcitepe), 23 kms from Eceabat
Y Beach is about 3.2kms from Krithia.
Time allowed: Three and a half hours

Krithia (1), completely destroyed in 1915 and rebuilt in the mid-1930s, is now a quiet rural community of 1,000 inhabitants with its goats, olive trees and cafes. It is a good place to buy a simple picnic, have a coffee or cold drink and plan your walk. It is recommended that you visit the small but fascinating **private museum (2)**, owned by Salim Mutlu, with artefacts found on the surrounding battlefields, including an amazing collection of Turkish grenades. It is always open! Soft drinks and snacks available and (only in desperation) a wc. The Allies never reached the village in force in 1915.

At the crossroads in the village, with several CWGC signs pointing

Trench map – 8th Army Corps, 28 December, 1915.

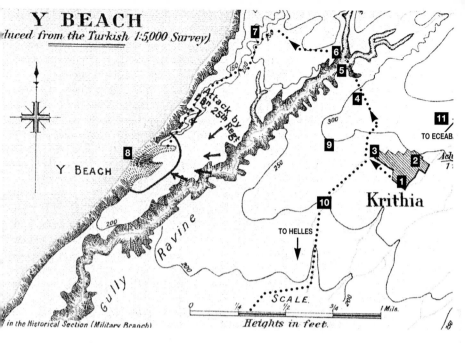

Y BEACH

duced from the Turkish 1:5,000 Survey)

Attack by 25th Reg[t].

Y BEACH

Ravine

Gully

Krithia

TO HELLES

SCALE.

TO ECEAB.

Ach
7.

in the Historical Section (Military Branch)

Heights in feet.

Y Beach Walk.
1. Krithia
2. Private museum
3. Fork in road
4. Son Ok monument/cemetery
5. Turkish soldier statue

6. Zigindere memorial/cemetery
7. Nuri Yamut memorial/cemetery
8. Y Beach
9. Lt Colonel Matthews' advance to Krithia
10. To Helles
11. To Eceabat

in various directions, face south, turn right and follow the *Twelve Tree Copse* sign. Continue for a short distance through the village outskirts until a **fork in the road (3)** is reached. Turn right and continue for about 500 m. The Turkish **Son Ok (Last Arrow) Monument and cemetery (4)** is located on the side of the road, built in 1948 to remember the dead of the Battles of Krithia. The inscription reads: *The gunners of a 12cm siege battery defeated the enemy at this point by a bayonet charge and so secured the Third Victory of Kirte(Krithia) 7 June 1915.*

Continue over the incline and you will be confronted with a huge **statue (5)** of a Turkish soldier on the left. In the bottom of the valley, close to the upper part of Gully Ravine, is **Zigindere Field Dressing Post Turkish**

Statue close to Zigindere
Field Dressing Post.

61

Y Beach: 'Nothing but a bloody cliff.'

Memorials and cemetery (6), originally the site of a Turkish field ambulance unit. The statues represent wounded soldiers from two Turkish regiments.

Continue along the track until the Turkish **Nuri Yamut Memorial and cemetery (7)** overlooking Fusilier Bluff and close to Gully Spur, is reached. This memorial commemorates 10,000 Turkish soldiers who died in the Gully Ravine battles from 26 June to 12 July 1915. The simple marble slab is inscribed *Sehidlik 1915* (To the Martyrs who died in Battle 1915).

There are two main ways of viewing Y Beach, which is one of the most inaccessible beaches on the Peninsula.

The first begins from this Memorial south along the cliff top with **Y Beach (8)**1200 m distant. There are no paths and no signs. The whole area is covered with prickly scrub and low bushes, and is very much off the beaten track. It is also partly on private property. Keep to the edge of the fields and away from the scrub on the edge of the clifftop and walk with care, pacing out the 1200 m. The route follows some of the British trench lines, now undistinguishable, such as Fifth Avenue, Western Mule Track and several small ravines are passed, such as Trolley, Border, Essex and Bruce's, until one reaches the area of Ghurka Bluff and Y Ravine. (Refer to Trench Map B dated 28.12.15) Along this clifftop is where the men of the 1/KOSB, the Plymouth Battalion and one company 2/SWB bivouacked all day after climbing with difficulty up the ravines after their unopposed landing. It was from here that two companies of Marines patrolled south east towards the 200 contour line about 1500 m distant.

However, with no fresh orders or reinforcements, a defensive position was taken up within 400 – 500 m of the cliff top above Y Beach. On reaching this position, one recalls that it was here that the persistent and fierce night attacks by the enemy took place, were courageously repulsed and it was from here that the force was 'unofficially' evacuated and the position finally abandoned. It was from this clifftop that Lieutenant Colonel Matthews and his adjutant **walked to within 500 m of a deserted Krithia on that lovely April morning (9)**, and did not encounter any of the enemy. Captain Cooper 1/KOSB also walked from this clifftop some distance inland and saw Morto Bay quite clearly.

On arriving above Y Beach, it is possible if one takes the utmost care and only if young and fit, to scramble and pick one's way down the steep slope towards the beach through the dense scrub and pine trees, but it is extremely difficult. Eventually one reaches a point where a good photograph can be taken. Descent to the beach itself is not recommended.

It is not difficult to imagine the hard and tiring work that would have been needed to drag all supplies, including ammunition, food and water to the top of these cliffs.

Return to the NuriYamut Memorial, then follow the same route back to Krithia.

A word of warning: If one visits Gully Beach, it possible to walk northward along the beach and reach Y Beach from there. This is not recommended. It is 2.5 kms of awkward and slow walking over large boulders and the return journey would take over three hours. It is also possible to reach the Y Beach area by walking up Gully Ravine, possibly an even longer walk.

But beware of snakes in the deep scrub!

Chapter Three

X BEACH – A DEFIANT STAND

On the western side of the Gallipoli Peninsula is a shallow indentation in the coast line. Barely noticeable from the sea, about one mile along the Aegean coastline from Tekke Burnu, it consists of a strip of sand about 200 yards long, about 9 yards wide and is at the foot of an steep escarpment some 50 to 100 feet high, sheltered from fire from the Asian shore of the Straits but exposed to fire from the direction of Krithia. This small beach was designated X Beach at the time of the landings on Gallipoli. The task of landing at X Beach was given to an initial covering force comprising of:

2/Royal Fusiliers – two companies and a machine gun section.

One platoon Anson Battalion, 2/Royal Naval Brigade, Royal Naval Division – as a working party.

Once the initial landing had taken place, and the beach secured, the follow up covering force would consist of 2/Royal Fusiliers – two companies and beach parties – 1/Border regiment and 1/Royal Inniskilling Fusiliers.

The Royal Fusiliers had three main tasks that day: to secure the beach and the cliff top; from the latter form a defensive flank running north east which was to offer protection for the execution of the main task, the capture of Hill 114 to the south; and then link up with the 1/Lancashire Fusiliers, who would be working in a northerly direction from W Beach.

With the rest of the 29th Division, who had left Avonmouth on 17 March, 1/Border Regiment had embarked on the SS *Andania* with 26 officers and 887 Ncos and men together with 1 officer and 115 other ranks in the *Duke of Edinburgh*. After a short stay in Malta they arrived in Alexandria on 28 March. Exercises took place here together with

Practising landings, Mudros harbour, Lemnos.

X Beach.

interminable practises of landing from boats. General Hamilton inspected both the 86 and 87 Brigades on 7 April, the day before the men sailed to Mudros Bay and wrote in his diary:

> *There was a strong wind blowing which tried to spoil the show, but could not – that infantry was too superb! Alexander, Hannibal, Caesar, Napoleon – not one of them had the handling of legionaires like these...If we don't win, I won't be able to put it on the men.*

The ships arrived in Mudros Bay on 12 April at 5.30 a.m. The following days were soon occupied by the commanders and staff in drawing up plans for putting the men and all the supplies on the Peninsula. The men relentlessly continued to practise getting up and down rope ladders and effecting landings of themselves and their equipment by small boats.

By 8.00 am on 24 April all the ships of the southern covering force

HMS *Implacable*, HMS *Euraylus* and HMS *Cornwallis*, were assembled at Tenedos, together with the collier *River Clyde* and three Cunarders.

The Official History portrays the activity of those last few hours:

During the day all ranks were engaged in preparing for the morrow's operation. Final conferences were held by the various Staffs, last orders issued, and tasks explained to subordinate leaders. Lighters were brought alongside the transports and filled with beach equipment, stores, and ammunition. Naval and military beach personnel were mustered, instructed in their duties, and distributed to their various ships. Picket boats, steam pinnaces, and pulling boats, dancing like corks in the tumbling sea, were collected from the warships and transports, and organised into eighteen tows, each with its crew. ....

About 10 pm the unwieldy flotilla of warships, transports, lighters, and small craft moved slowly out from the anchorage, speed and course being so arranged as to bring the ships west of Tekke Burnu about an hour before daylight. There was a bright moon; the breeze had died away; the sea was a sheet of shining silver.

To the south were the main body of the 29th Division approaching from Mudros, whose deep anchorage they had left at 4.00 pm on 24 April.

By 3.30 am 25 April the moon had set and in deep darkness HMS *Implacable*, HMS *Euryalus* and Fleet Sweeper No. 1 reached their positions about two miles from the Beaches, X, W and V. In the tense

HMS *Implacable* steaming towards X Beach.

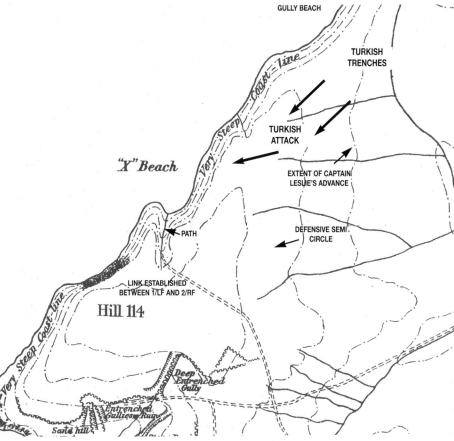

X Beach, situation as at 25 April, 1915.

atmosphere the troops were woken up and given breakfast before being mustered on deck. Just as day dawned softly, at about 4.00 am, the men filed down gangways from their ships and filled the waiting little boats in complete silence.

The Official History continues:

> *The morning was absolutely still. The garrison of the peninsula gave no sign of life. A thick veil of mist hung motionless over the beaches. The sea was smooth as glass.*

Just before 6.00 am on 25 April 1915, HMS *Implacable* sent off one company 1/LF, destined for W Beach, accompanied by Brigadier General Hare, Officer Commanding Covering Force and continued around the coast, firing on X Beach with her four tows of Royal Fusiliers alongside.

The bombardment of X Beach by HMS *Implacable*, commanded by Captain Hughes Lockyer RN, with her 12 inch guns, was very effective. Something of an individualist, in 1893 the then Lieutenant

Lockyer had taken part in secret surveys by HMS *Fearless* at Lemnos. He and his surveying party had been made to work around the clock, Sundays included, by Captain AC Corry RN. During this time, Lockyer had named four hills around the harbour mouth at Mudros Yam, Yrroc, Eb and Denmad. When these unusual names were challenged by his captain, Lockyer gave an explanation which was accepted. However, it had not occurred to Captain Corry to read the names backwards!

HMS *Implacable* had arrived from W Beach and managed to get to within 500 yards of the shore, closer than any of the other ships involved in the bombardment. She had also been able to maintain her fire as she accompanied her tows as close to the shore as possible. When this point had been reached HMS *Implacable* continued to fire over the cliff tops until the precise moment the boats grounded.

Sir Ian Hamilton wrote admiringly,

> *About 6am HMS* Implacable, *with boldness much admired by the Army, stood quite close in to the beach, firing very rapidly with every gun she could bring to bear.*

Captain Lockyer's initiative had a most encouraging effect on the men, and their morale was high as they approached the beach in their vulnerable boats. Midshipman Stanley Norfolk RN summed up the atmosphere that early morning:

> *I have never forgotten the impression which that never to be forgotten run in to the beach made on me, and even more on the soldiers in my boat. They were simply enthralled with the sight of the cliff face being literally blown away by the ship's guns and the spectacle of the ship steaming in firing was magnificent. I think it is no exaggeration to say that the morale of the troops in the boats went up two to three hundred per cent on that account. I remember it was a beastly cold morning and when the troops embarked from the ship they looked (and evidently felt) anything but heroes. The change in their attitude towards what lay ahead during that short run in alongside the ship was quite phenomenal. It was a complete revelation to me, and I have often felt that if the other landings had been similarly conducted there would have been a very different tale to tell.*

Here at X Beach, the possibility of a landing or assault was not considered by the enemy. There was just a small Turkish piquet/section of twelve men from the 3/26 Regiment to guard this section of the coast in trenches that ran along the top of the cliff. No wire had been erected.

At 6.30 am on 25 April 1915, with the small Turkish guard

stupefied by the *Implacable's* fire, the first two companies 2/RF as well as Battalion HQ and the machine gun section had reached the summit of the cliff without a single casualty. However, as soon as they advanced from the cliff top, they met Turkish resistance in the form of a company of Turkish reserves who had been bivouacking nearby. One company had been sent to reinforce Sedd El Bahr and the other to W Beach. It was this latter company, from the 2/26 Regiment, which now faced the 2/RF.

As Lieutenant Colonel Newenham and his one and a half companies moved across a line of Turkish trenches, in the direction of Hill 114, he ordered Captain Leslie and his company to strike out north eastwards and form the required defensive position. However, when they were some 800 yards from the cliff top, Captain Leslie met the full force of the Turkish Reserve company, and the advance faltered. Captain Leslie, a regular soldier from Co. Monaghan, was killed very shortly afterwards. His name is on the Helles Memorial.

In the meantime the remaining two companies of 2/RF, together with naval and military beach personnel, heavy equipment and reserve ammunition, were ashore by 7.30 am.

At 7.15 am disembarkation had also commenced from the SS *Andania*, with most of 1/Border Regiment going onto Mine Sweeper No. 6. A total strength of 950 men were then transferred to smaller boats. A few of the Battalion (51 in number) remained on the *Duke of Edinburgh* and *Mercian*.

The first part of the 29th Division's main body, 1/Border Regiment and 1/Royal Inniskilling Fusiliers, began to land about 9.00 am with Brigadier General Marshall (GOC 87 Brigade), commanding the main

The Royal Inniskilling Fusiliers landing under fire, 25 April 1915.

body, along with his Brigade Headquarters. These two battalions were to form the Divisional Reserve.

This landing was described by Major Cuthbert Lucas as follows:

> *It was a bright sunny morning, dead calm sea, not a shot fired. I had a bag in one hand, a coat over my arm, and was assisted down a plank from the boat by an obliging sailor, so that I should not wet my boots. The only thing missing was the Hotel.*

The troops, relieved to be on 'terra firma' at last, formed up below the crest of the cliff and awaited their orders, which did not arrive until about midday. Their allotted task was then to support the attack of the 2/RF on Hill 114.

But although the element of surprise at X Beach, together with the point blank firing of the guns of HMS *Implacable,* had enabled the landing to be effected without any serious opposition and the first objective gained, the difficulties began as soon as attempts were made to consolidate the position with reinforcements.

The Anson Battalion were soon ordered to construct a path up the cliff and a wireless station was established on the beach.

Brigadier General Marshall's own position was rather ambivalent. His Brigade had been split.The 2/SWB and 1/KOSB were on S and Y Beaches, and the other two battalions, 1/Border and 1/RIF were in Divisional Reserve, and thus were all out of his immediate control. The 2/RF at X Beach were not under his orders but under the direct control of the OC Covering Force (Brigadier-General Hare). The fact that the troops with him were not strictly speaking under his orders placed him in rather a quandry. Although by mid-morning both Brigadier General Hare and Major Frankland had become casualties, he was uncertain of what he should do and decided to wait for the men landing at W and V Beaches to come up and join him, which meant he would have no influence outside the small area of the landing at X Beach.

In the meantime Lieutenant Colonel Newenham and his men, after some difficulty, eventually reached the summit of Hill 114

at 11.00 am. For most of this action, the soldiers were cheered on by the men of HMS *Implacable* as if they were watching a football match. But Fleet Surgeon Forrester RN on board the battleship was hit by a rifle bullet and killed. He had been educated in Glasgow and enlisted in the Royal Navy as Surgeon in November 1898. He joined his ship on February 11 1914 and is now commemorated on the Chatham Memorial.

Brigadier General Marshall then received a worried message from 2/RF as he reached the top of the cliff, saying that they were being determinedly attacked by Turks from Gully Beach. Unless help was sent, their left flank would be turned and they would be driven back to the beach. So at about 12.30 pm he sent some reinforcements from 1/Border Regiment under Captain Morton, with 2 maxim guns, but all the time the men were being pushed back towards X Beach. The murderous fire increased, sweeping over the cliff top. Further reinforcements of 1/Border were ordered to charge the enemy who were now within about 400 yards of the edge of the cliff. Despite having to face such a terrifying hail of bullets, this attack was carried out with great gallantry and grim use of bayonets. As a result the British advance was continued for almost 600 yards eastwards. It was during this time that two officers of 1/Border became casualties, Lieutenant James killed and Lieutenant Bartholomew mortally wounded.

Road construction at X Beach.

On the right flank, matters were a little better and the advance pushed the Turks back for at least 600 yards. However, they were not pursued. Then Major Vaughan, Second in Command 1/Border was killed, at the age of 47.

Major Charles Davies Vaughan DSO, a Welshman born in Cardiganshire, was one of six brothers, all of whom were in the Royal Navy or the army. He had seen action in various parts of the far flung British Empire, having been commissioned into the Border Regiment in 1889 and promoted to Lieutenant in 1891, Captain in April 1898 and Brevet-Major in November 1900, and gazetted Major in August 1910. He served with the 2/Border Regiment in India and in the Waziristan Campaign 1894-5, served on the North West Frontier in 1897-8 and went with them to South Africa. He was severely wounded on January 20, 1900, during the attempts to relieve Ladysmith, and fought on the Tugela Heights, Pieter's Hill, Orange Free State, Transvaal and later Cape Colony. He acquitted himself well, being mentioned in despatches twice on 10 September 1901 and 29 July 1902. As well as the Queen's Medal with five bars and King's Medal, he was awarded the DSO in recognition of services during the operations in South Africa. At the conclusion of hostilities in South Africa he stayed on in various posts, including that of District Commissioner, until 1906. He sailed with his Regiment as Second in Command. At the time he was killed he had been married for just 18 months.

Major C D Vaughan DSO
1/Border Regiment.

The original graves of Major Vaughan and Lieutenant Bartholomew, 1/Border Regiment, on X Beach (right hand corner).

1/Royal Irish Fusiliers had landed by about 1.00 pm. The line had been re-established and eventually a beachhead around X Beach secured with the assistance of the remainder of the 1/Border and the 1/RIF.

41 year old Lieutenant Colonel Francis Jones, Commanding Officer of 1/RIF, encouraged and led his men with distinction at this stage. From Mallow Co. Cork he joined his regiment in 1885. The loss of his experience proved to be a great blow when he was seriously wounded on 2 May 1915, and died of wounds on 5 May on board Caledonia en route to an Egyptian hospital. He was buried at sea, and is commemorated on the Helles Memorial.

Lieutenant Colonel Newenham, 2/RF was then advised he was now in charge of the Covering Force as the Brigadier General had been wounded, but shortly afterwards he himself became a casualty.

At about 1.00 pm Brigadier General Marshall still had not heard from Divisional HQ. He saw that Hills 141 and 138 were still in the hands of the Turkish Army. He felt he could not

Lieutenant Colonel F G Jones, died of wounds on 5 May on board *Caledonia* en route to an Egyptian hospital. He was buried at sea, an example of which is shown above.

commit his two battalions (1/Border and 1/RIF) without orders, so he felt he had little choice but to protect X Beach. At 3.43 pm he signalled to Divisional Headquarters that he would dig in at X Beach on his present position and wait for the main advance from Sedd el Bahr, along with his two battalions and the men from 2/RF. The men began digging in.

During the afternoon Major Vaughan and Lieutenant James were buried on X Beach but they were later re-interred in Pink Farm Cemetery together with Lieutenant Bartholomew.

Just before dark a complete defensive semi-circle had been established with a radius of 800 yards from the landing beach; and the line re-organised. Still no contact had been made with any of the other beaches and so, in common with remainder of the attacking force, X

Beach force remained on the defensive all day despite being superior in numbers.

Brigadier General Marshall made repeated requests earlier for permission to advance to Y beach, as he could hear sounds of sustained fighting from that area, but nothing was forthcoming from Divisional HQ until 8:00 pm that evening. Conflicting orders meant that it was too late to contact Y Beach and later GOC 87 Brigade was ordered to stay put until the next day.

There was a mistaken belief at Divisional Headquarters that a continuous line now existed from Y to X Beaches despite the fact that, for a period of about twelve hours, 29th Division Headquarters had received a succession of messages from various different sources asking for assistance and pointing out the increasingly serious situation at Y Beach.

26 APRIL

A prolonged and heavy attack by the Turks developed from midnight and continued unabated until dawn, but the Turks suffered considerable loss and retired before daylight. For most of that day there was no other serious fighting, but the troops had to contend with annoying and accurate sniper fire which inflicted a large number of casualties among the ration parties and messengers. At one point snipers tried to draw the fire of 1/Border by shooting at their trenches from 300 - 400 yards away, but to no avail. Strict orders had been given that no one was to fire unless ordered to do so by an officer.

27 APRIL

The British position remained virtually unchanged and the men continued to hold the original line whilst sniping continued. The hard pressed men around X Beach were told the good news that Hill 138 and the Castle had been captured at last.

The 1/Border Battalion War Diary records the following remarks:

A field battery opened on the enemy as they retired in the direction of Achi Baba. All sniping at once ceased and all pressure on the line by the enemy was at once relaxed. Parties were sent out to reconnoitre the places from which most of the sniping had come and it was found on investigation that the enemy had suffered severely and from thirty to forty dead were counted in the valley.

The 1/Border War Diary continues:

This order necessitated the digging of fresh trenches by C and

Supplies being landed on a congested X Beach.

*D Coys, and the men being thoroughly tired out with hard work
and hard fighting, the process was naturally slow but was
however safely accomplished by midnight. The enemy was
quiescent during the night.*

AFTERMATH

The operations on X Beach had began well. The inspiring effect of
12 inch guns firing at point blank range at the shore, the successful
landing with very few casualties, the first objective being seized
without difficulty and the beachhead secured for the landing of the
main body, was encouraging. However it has to be remembered that
any advance had been met with stubborn resistance and significant
counter attacks had to be repelled.

Perhaps if a larger force had been employed at X Beach there might
well have been a different outcome; or if there had been a positive
advance in a south easterly direction from X Beach on Hills 138 and
141, this would have relieved the pressure on both W and V Beaches.
But hindsight is a wonderful concept and the Allies were handicapped
by the lack of appreciation of the ground. Morto Bay, just over two
miles way, can be seen from the cliff top and it would have been
possible for visual communication, e.g. by heliograph, between the
forces at both Y and S, but this was not considered.

The Official History summarises the position succinctly:

As it was, the troops who first landed at X were probably too much engaged with carrying out the task allotted to them to give even a thought to the boats which must have been clearly visible in Morto Bay. It is even doubtful whether many of the officers at X had been told where S Beach was, even if they knew that a landing was to take place there.

WALK NO 2: X BEACH

There are two main possibilities for exploring X Beach, about 30kms from Eceabat. It can also be done in conjunction with Y and W Beaches very easily.

Starting Point: Sedd El Bahr (2.7 kms) or Krithia (5kms)
1) From **Sedd El Bahr (1)**, follow the main Krithia road out of the village, take the left fork at the junction and travel across the Peninsula with the site of **Lieutenant Colonel Doughty Wylie's grave (2)** (See V Beach Walk) on your right, and V and W beaches on your left. You will pass **Lancashire Landing Cemetery (3)** on your left. 1500 metres further, after the road bends to the right, you will find the track

1. **Sedd El Bahr**
2. **Lt. Colonel Doughty-Wylie's grave**
3. **Lancashire Landing Cemetery**
4. **X Beach**
5. **Twelve Copse Cemetery**
6. **Pink Farm Cemetery**

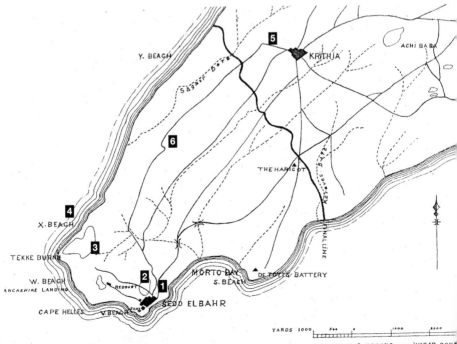

to **X Beach (4)** on the left hand side of the road.

2) From Krithia, take the road signposted **Twelve Tree Copse CWGC and Pink Farm CWGC**. X Beach is about 4 kms from **Twelve Tree Copse CWGC (4)**, which was on the final allied Front Line at the end of the Gallipoli Campaign. Continue on the coast road past **Pink Farm CWGC (6)**.

X Beach (1) will be found on the right hand side of the road. In 1915 the trench running parallel to the road was known as Longitudinal 1. If you are driving, you will need to be careful not to miss **the turning (2)** to the rough track leading to the Beach. There are no signposts. The

1. X Beach
2. Turning to beach
3. Hill 114
4. Extent of Captain Leslie's advance
5. Bakery Beach
6. Pink Farm Cemetery
7. Aprox. position of defensive semi circle end 25 April

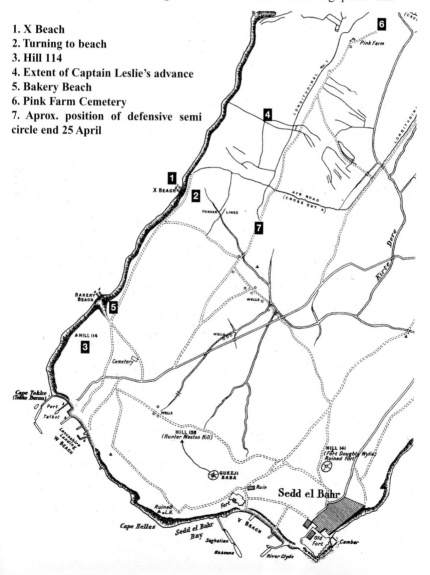

view from the cliffs above the beach here are excellent, a fact that was not known at the time of the landings, as the maps available were very inaccurate and there had been no possibility of a reconnaissance. From here it is possible to look ahead and note how the ground rises to **Hill 114 (3)**, with the road bending to the left. The Helles Memorial just below Hill 138 stands out. Hill 141, with its water tower and the two distinctive cypress trees at Lieutenant Colonel Doughty Wylie's grave, can be seen clearly.

Walk down on to the beach. **X Beach**, also known as Implacable Landing, was the scene of one of the more successful landings on 25 April. The track today is the remains of the path built by the Anson Battalion on the day of the landings. Standing on the rugged beach, one can only try to imagine HMS *Implacable* steaming in, guns blazing and blasting some of the almost sheer cliff face away and then firing over the cliff top. Walk from the beach up the path to the top of the cliff from where the British troops met with Turkish resistance. **Captain Leslie and his men** were ordered to the left whilst others pushed on straight ahead and to the right. Their **advance was held up after some 800 yards (4)** and then they were pushed back, the Turks eventually reaching to within 400 yards of the cliff top and even at one stage were almost at the cliff edge itself. They were eventually pushed back about 600 yards to the east.

As you walk along the coast road today towards the hill, one can appreciate how exposed those men would have felt. However, by dusk the troops here eventually secured and defended a semi circle with an 800 yard radius from the cliff top **(7)**.

The assault on **Hill 114 (3)** met eventual success and it was taken by 11.00am when some troops of 2/Royal Fusiliers met up with the

X Beach today.

1/Lancashire Fusiliers and secured the position, although it remained a weak point for much of the day. Looking across the peaceful fields today it is hard to imagine the continuous rifle and machine gun fire maintained throughout that night by the British troops to keep the enemy at bay. The following day, whilst the main body of the enemy had retired, Turkish snipers used trees as cover, some only about 300-400 yards away.

Continue in a southerly direction, past Hill 114 towards W Beach. After about 600 yards you will note a slight indentation in the clifftop. Below on the right hand side is **Bakery Beach (5)** where the first fresh bread was produced on 21 May. The steep track is overgrown and access to the beach is not possible.

Cemeteries close to X Beach:

TWELVE TREE COPSE CEMETERY

The majority of the 3,359 casualties commemorated here were from later battles. However, Captain Harold Clayton, who landed on W Beach on 25 April and was killed on 4 June in or near Gully Spur, is buried here (SM B.8). The original pine trees were destroyed by shellfire during the campaign, but twelve representative pines have been planted since.

PINK FARM CEMETERY

With 602 burials, the cemetery takes its name from the red soil nearby.

Lieutenant (Captain) James (Special Memorial 44) and Lieutenant Bartholomew, (Special Memorial 122), 1/Border Regiment, are buried here, killed after landing at X Beach. Another great loss to that same Regiment would have been the death of Major G C Brooke, MID, who was killed on 28 April (Special memorial 127). Major Vaughan, 1/Border Regiment, also lies here (Special Memorial 109).

Packs of dogs, ostensibly guarding sheep and goats, roam in this vicinity and near the entrance to Gully Ravine, so care needs to be taken, particularly if no shepherd can be seen.

Pink Farm Cemetery Helles.

Chapter Four

W BEACH – SIX VICTORIA CROSSES BEFORE BREAKFAST

W Beach is on the south west promontory of the Gallipoli Peninsula. With its white sand, shallow water and enveloping cliffs giving shelter from westerly winds, it is today probably one of the more natural and unspoilt beaches on the Peninsula. To the sound of bells tinkling from a flock of sheep close by, the peaceful walk from the dirt track between Hill 114 and the sand dunes to the beach is hardly redolent of the ill-fated and heart-rending events that occurred here.

Standing on the edge of the water, with the sea gently lapping over the rusty relics of piers and reddish brown remains of ships' hulls, one can still see the same yellow cliffs on either side of the long beach, the same dunes, covered in wild flowers in springtime, and some trench lines on top of the cliffs, shallower now but still visible. Vestiges of prosaic items used during the campaign lie on the ground – metal buckets, entrenching tools - together with more sinister items – such as pieces of shell, spent bullets, or a piece of rifle. It is a place to quietly explore, undisturbed, and to reflect on those momentous events and the outstanding courage that was exhibited all those years ago.

It was the task of 1/Lancashire Fusiliers, 86 Brigade, 29th Division, VIII Corps, to effect a landing on W Beach on 25 April, to attack Hills 114 and 138, and eventually link up with the Royal Fusiliers from X Beach to the west and with other troops of 29th Division on V Beach to the east.

1/LF were commanded by Lieutenant Colonel Ormond. They arrived in Lemnos on 10 April 1915. They had sailed on HT *Caledonia* from Alexandria on 8 April with 27 officers, 930 other ranks and seven days supplies, including two days' iron rations, 200 rounds of ammunition per man, tools and signalling equipment, but no transport.

For almost three weeks the men, as thousands of other soldiers had done, practised transferring themselves, stores, ammunition and machine guns from the ships to wooden rowing boats (or cutters, as they were known). They worked out that it took 35 minutes to load 830 men into 22 cutters, which meant there would be about 35 - 40 men per boat. An extract from the War Diary of the 1/LF indicates the constant and laborious efforts made to prepare for the imminent landing:

Lemnos

April 12 Practised landing men into boats by day and by night
April 14 Practised transferring from ship to boats day and night
April 15 Practised landings in ships boats manned by bluejackets
Took machine guns and ammunition
April 16 Practised landings by half battalions
April 17 Landed on Lemnos island and route marched

April 19 788 all ranks transferred in 6 tows of 4 cutters each to HMS Euryalus for practise in mustering ready for eventual disembarkation

The need for the most careful but urgent preparation was paramount. As John Masefield wrote in his book *Gallipoli*:

They were going to land on a foodless cliff, five hundred miles from a store, in a place and at a season in which the sea's rising might cut them from supply. They had to take with them all things - munitions, guns, entrenching tools, sandbags,

Allied transports at Lemnos, where preparations were made for the landings.

81

provisions, clothing, medical stores, hospital equipment, mules, horses, fodder, even water to drink...These military supplies had to be arranged in boats and lighters in such a way that they might be thrust ashore with many thousands of men in all haste but without confusion..

The weather cleared up considerably on 23 April and a beautiful haze fell over the hills of Lemnos. The great ships were crowded in the bay of Mudros Harbour, surrounded by picket boats busily moving back and forward on their last minute errands. 1/LF left Lemnos at 5.30 pm that evening.

Ship after ship, crammed with soldiers who excitedly pressed along the rails of the decks, moved slowly and majestically out of the protection of the harbour, with the surrounding hills echoing to thousands and thousands of voices cheering, as the men swung their caps exultantly and the sailors joined in the fervour.

By 8.00 am on the morning of 24 April 1915 all the ships of the southern covering force had assembled at Tenedos, just a few miles from the Asiatic shore, including HMS *Cornwallis*, HMS *Euryalus* and HMS *Implacable* and the collier SS *River Clyde*, together with fleet sweeps, trawlers, lighters and tugs. It seemed that the Turks had become so accustomed to naval activity that they did not pay much notice to this great gathering.

At 6.00 pm. on 24 April 25 officers and 918 other ranks were transferred to HMS *Euryalus* in readiness for the landing on 25 April. By 24 April Lieutenant Colonel Ormond had been taken ill and Major Bishop took command.

The Turkish army had made the cove, some 350 yards in length, 15 to 40 yards wide, with steep cliffs on either side, into a death trap. W Beach lay between Tekke Burnu and Cape Helles and in the centre were a series of sand dunes which appeared to offer an easy approach to the ridge which overlooked the sea. A belt of barbed wire, three feet in height, ran close to the water's edge along the whole length of the sheltered bay and the proposed landing area. This had been untouched by the preceding naval bombardment.

Trip wires had been placed in the water a few yards from the shore. Land mines were put on the beach and in the water. Short lengths of trench had been made on the summits of the cliffs on either side of the beach and on the slopes facing seawards; and these had not been damaged. Also Brigadier General Hare was certain that two Turkish machine guns were firing from the right flank of W Beach when he landed, but this was later refuted by the Turks.

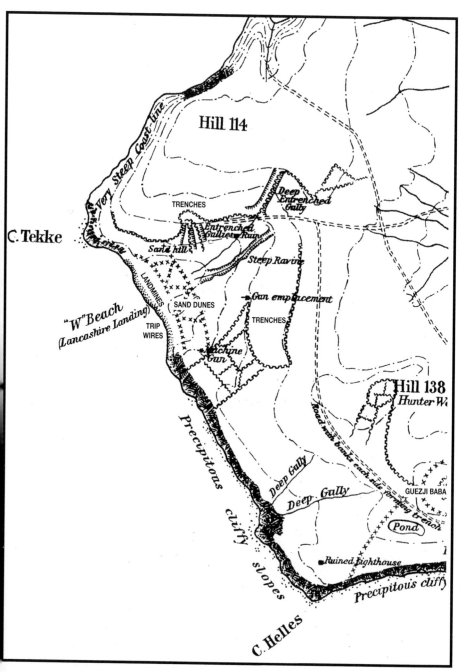

W Beach defences: 25 April 1915.

The low ridge, which commanded a view of the centre of the beach, was itself overlooked by further trenches on low hills to the south west and the north east. The closer of the two redoubts on Hill 138 was about 600 yards distant. Strong barbed wire defences surrounded both the redoubts and the approach was completely exposed, with no cover afforded to advancing troops. Another serious obstacle was the wide band of wire which ran from the most southerly redoubt to a point on the cliffs near the old lighthouse. One overriding difficulty was the fact that it would be impossible to advance from W Beach to V Beach unless the Redoubt on Hill 138 was captured. Perhaps because of these formidable defences the Turks had only placed one company of infantry from the 3/26 Regiment at W Beach at that time. The objectives for that day were:

A Company (led by Captain Haworth) and B Company (led by Captain Shaw) and with the battalion machine guns, were to attack the trench and Redoubt on Hill 138.

C Company, with Captain Willis, was to capture the trenches guarding the centre and left of the beach, and assist the Royal Fusiliers in the attack on Hill 114, the high point to the south west of the Peninsula.

2 platoons of D Company under Major Adams were to be in reserve under Tekke Burnu, together with the Commanding Officer, Major Bishop, and the Adjutant, Captain Cuthbert Bromley. The remainder of D Company would arrive on HMS *Implacable,* together with Headquarters Company.

As John Masefield wrote in his contemporary account, *Gallipoli,* published in 1917:

W Beach looking east. Scene of advance of A and B Companies 1/Lancashire Fusiliers.

No army in history has made a more heroic attack; no army in history has been set such a task. No other body of men in any modern war has been called upon to land over mined and wired waters under the crossfire of machine guns.

Sunday April 25 1915

At 4.00 am, some distance out at sea, the troops transferred to the cutters and were towed by steam picket boats towards the shore. It was a beautiful morning, and the sea was oily, calm as a millpond. As noted in Geoffrey Moorhouse's *Hell's Foundations:*

Everyone who survived the next few hours was to remember this perfection of Nature at peace for as long as he lived.

What a contrast to the carnage, noise, confusion and death that was to follow! HMS *Euryalus* relentlessly bombarded the Turkish positions as part of the naval support. The British fleet had agreed to commence its bombardment of the southern end of the Peninsula at 5.00 am with the intention that this should continue for half an hour, when the fire would be lifted and the tows would go ahead. Soon after 4.30 am the men were 2,000 yards off W Beach and the flotillas were towed in with the troops sitting tense and silent, staring at the dark shape of the land in front of them.

Those of a thoughtful mentality knew for a fact that certain death awaited some, either by machine gun fire, a blast of a shell or a stray bullet; others would be wounded and would have to suffer permanent disability for the remainder of their lives. Others, who perhaps could be considered the lucky ones, would be found perspiring in foul trenches, with little rest, meagre rations and a poor water supply, having to live and work under the blazing sun of the Peninsula during the day and suffer the cold at night, in exposed conditions amongst a fearful number of huge flies. But perhaps for the most part a sense of adventure and of going into battle with their friends overcame any sense of foreboding. They were soon awakened into reality.

When the small wooden boats were fifty yards from the beach, they were set free and slowly and laboriously rowed ashore by crews commanded by midshipmen. There was no sound, no movement, not a sign of life, just the soft sound of the muffled oars in the water and the lapping of the waves.

At about 5.30 am, just before the first boat grounded, the Lancashire Fusiliers heard the vicious crack of rifle and machine gun fire and a hurricane of lead swept over the Battalion. The covering bombardment from HMS *Euryalus* and HMS *Swiftsure* had lifted

An arists impression of troops being disembarked whilst under covering fire from friendly warships.

some ten minutes before to allow for the landing, and this had afforded the Turkish defenders ample time and opportunity to prepare for it. Evidently the Turks had been given the strictest instructions not to open fire until the enemy were within a hundred yards range.

Gallantly led by their officers, the 1/LF jumped into the sea, only to find themselves waist deep in water. They hurled themselves ashore as best they could with their heavy packs, weighing over 80 pounds, and rifle. Many died or fell wounded as they sat helplessly in the boats, drowned in the water as they were pulled down by their packs, or were killed by deadly accurate machine gun fire as they struggled to the beach. Captain Richard Willis, commanding C Company, recollected the scene with great clarity later:

> The sea was like glass, but as the picket boats drew off to get into formation our boats heeled over dangerously, and one of the men remarked to the cox, 'I 'listed to get killed, not to get drowned'. As the tows got to a safe distance from the ships the shelling began again, the guns lifting their fire as we approached the shore. When the water began to get shallow the picket boats called out 'Slip', for the tow ropes to be cast off, and we began to approach the shore under the oars of the naval ratings. There were five to each boat. Not a sign of life was to be seen on the Peninsula in front of us. It might have been a deserted land we were nearing in our little boats. Then crack! The stroke oar of my boat fell forward, to the angry astonishment of his mates. The

signal for the massacre had been given: rapid fire, machine guns and deadly accurate sniping opened from the cliffs above, and soon the casualties included the rest of the crew and many men. The timing of the ambush was perfect; we were completely exposed and helpless in our slow-moving boats, just target practice for the concealed Turks, and within a few minutes only half of the thirty men in my boat were left alive. We were now 100 yards from the shore, and I gave the order 'Overboard'. We scrambled out into some four feet of water, and some of the boats with their cargo of dead and wounded floated away on the currents, still under fire from the snipers. With this unpromising start the advance began. Many were hit in the sea, and no response was possible, for the enemy was in trenches well above our heads'

Captain Willis was seen to stand up in the boat and yell out above the din of the machine guns and bullets, *Come on C Company! Remember Minden!* which really inspired the assaulting troops. (In August 1759 the Regiment, together with other British troops and German allies, had withstood three French cavalry charges and put both the cavalry and the French infantry to rout whilst attacking the bridge at Minden.)

Because the boats had grounded in such unexpectedly deep water, the machine guns could not be landed. Some men tried to swim ashore, losing three of the guns in the process. The fourth gun was landed with them later that morning. The next formidable obstacle which faced

1/Lancashire Fusiliers landing at W Beach. Captain 'Walking Stick' Willis in the centre.

them was the three foot high, unyielding, barbed wire entanglement on the shoreline. Still waist high in the water, they desperately hacked at the wire, oblivious of the unrelenting fusillade being poured upon them.

One man in desperation tore up the stakes with his bare hands as blood poured from seven different wounds in his body.

Others had wire cutters, but had no chance to use them as they were mown down by the continued furious machine gun and rifle fire coming from the left, the centre and the right of the beach. The *War Diary* of 1/LF tersely deals with the landing in four brief sentences:

Gallipoli April 25 5.30 am Landed – under heavy fire from machine guns and rifles from cliffs. Heavy casualties. Several men hit in boats and in water before getting ashore. Barbed wire entanglements near water's edge.

It should perhaps be noted that there is an apparent discrepancy in the exact timing of the Landing. The *War Diary* of the 1/LF, signed by the Commanding Officer, Major Bishop, states 5.30 am, whilst the Official History by Brigadier General Aspinal-Oglander indicates that it was a little later, some time after 6.00 am. (The fact that watches and compasses were in many cases rendered useless during the landing may go some way in accounting for this small difference.)

Captain Richard Willis continued his graphic story:

We toiled through the water towards the sandy beach, but here another trap was awaiting us, for the Turks had cunningly concealed a trip wire just below the surface of the water, and on the beach itself were a number of land mines, and a deep belt of rusty wire extended across the landing place. Machine guns, hidden in caves at the end of the amphitheatre of cliffs, enfiladed this. Our wretched men were ordered to wait behind this wire for the wire cutters to cut a pathway through. They were shot in helpless batches while they waited, and could not even use their rifles in retaliation, since the sand and the sea had clogged their action. One Turkish sniper in particular took a heavy toll at very close range until I forced open the bolt of a rifle with the heel of my boot and closed his career with the first shot, but the heap of empty cartridges round him testified to the damage he had done.

Captain Harold Shaw, B Company, later wrote a grim personal account of his experiences:

About 100 yards from the beach the enemy opened fire and bullets came thick all around, splashing up the water. as soon as I felt the boat touch, I dashed over the side into three feet of water and rushed for the barbed wire entanglements on the beach: it must have been only three feet high or so, because I got over it amidst a perfect storm of lead and made for cover, sand dunes on the other side, and got good cover. I then found that only Maunsell and two men had followed me. On the right of me on the cliff was a line of Turks taking pot shots at us. I looked back. There was only one soldier between me and the wire, and a whole line in a row at the edge of the sands. The sea behind was absolutely crimson, and you could hear the groans through the rattle of musketry .

Captain Thomas Bowyer Lane Maunsell, born 18 April 1882 in Nova Scotia in Canada, was the son of Surgeon General Thomas Maunsell and had been educated at the Oratory School, Edgbaston. Commissioned in 1901 at the age of 19, he had a promising military career in front of him. He was killed shortly afterwards on the beach and is buried in Lancashire Landing Cemetery (Plot I.100).

Captain Clayton wrote of his experiences:

I got up to my waist in water, tripped over a rock and went under, got up and made for the shore and lay down by the barbed wire. There was a man there before me shouting for wire-cutters. I got mine out but could not make the slightest impression. The front of the wire by now was a thick mass of men, the majority of whom never moved again.

Captain Willis recalled later :

An astonishing sight was now seen: soldiers on the beach, under close fire of the enemy, getting out brushes and oil to clean their rifles, a job which would not have been necessary if the company commander's request for rifle covers had been listened to.

Eventually, a passage was cut through the wire and small groups of troops managed to reach the sand dunes in the centre of the beach and capture the Turkish trenches. Thus, despite appalling casualties, C Company managed to achieve their first objective. Captain Willis remembered that when he looked back he saw a considerable number of men still lying on the beach below, behind the wire, apparently waiting for the order to advance.

I ordered one of my company to signal down 'No enemy in sight' to bring them on, but he evidently thought I was mad, and signalled 'Enemy in sight' instead, whereupon Lance Corporal Grimshaw, who was near, laughingly threatened him with extra drill, and he gave the correct signal. But right or wrong, signals did not matter, for I suddenly realized those men would never

*advance again. They were all dead – four officers and seventy
five men fallen in one line as they came under the fire of the
machine guns.*

On the far left of W Beach, Brigadier-General Hare, the Commander
of the Covering Force, who had insisted on landing with the first trip
of tows with his Staff against the wishes of the Divisional Commander,
noted that the water was calm enough for boats to land safely on a
ledge of rock to the north of the bay. He ordered his own boat's crew,
together with the remaining boats from HMS *Implacable,* to follow
him. He could be seen standing up, shouting and gesticulating to the
tows to land towards this more sheltered left hand side of the beach.
The shore was reached without any opposition. He personally led a few
Lancashire Fusiliers and his Brigade Major, Major Frankland,
(1/Royal Dublin Fusiliers) to the top of the cliff, where he occupied an
empty trench. He then found that he was within thirty yards of the
Turkish defensive position on the northern flank. Grabbing a rifle,
Major Frankland shot two of the enemy and the remainder fled.

As the rest of the Lancashire Fusiliers breathlessly reached the top
of the cliff, Major Frankland urged them to link up with the General's
small party. The Battalion Adjutant, Captain Cuthbert Bromley, a
strong and fit officer who had been a physical training instructor,
staunchly and energetically supported the Brigade Major, leading
small groups of men, without their own leaders, forward, shouting
encouragement to those who seemed to be flagging, all the time quite
oblivious of the constant Turkish fire. Brigadier-General Hare, together
with his Brigade Major and a small party of signallers, led a
reconnaissance in the direction of Hill 114 and to link up with the
Royal Fusiliers on X Beach. It must be considered that Brigadier-
General Hare, Commander of the Covering Force, should not perhaps
have attempted to reach and take initial objectives. The inevitable
happened and his small party had gone only 200 yards when fire came
from Hill 114 and Hare was severely wounded and evacuated from the
Peninsula, all at about 7.15 am. This loss was to have an adverse effect
on the landings.

Major Frankland immediately sent word to Lieutenant Colonel
Newenham, commanding the Royal Fusiliers and at that time
advancing on Hill 114 from X Beach, that he, Colonel Newenham, was
now in charge of the Covering Force. Major Frankland, once he was
satisfied everything was in hand, then returned to the beach at about
7.30 am with a view to organise an attack on Hill 138 and to endeavour
to establish his headquarters at the lighthouse. But it was not long

before Colonel Newenham was seriously wounded and the situation became very confused.

Eventually, by unstinting effort, more paths were cut through the wire on the beach as the fierce fire began to diminish. On the right hand side of the beach men charged towards the low cliff which overlooked the southern end of the beach with bayonets fixed. They had no choice, as their rifles had jammed with sand and seawater.

Captain Haworth, together with the remnants of his Company, was hurled violently back by a blast just as he reached the summit of the cliff face by what he thought at first was a land mine, although it later appeared to have been a shell from the Royal Navy that had exploded on top of the cliff. Soon, despite the most terrible losses, a line had been gained on the beach and the area made safe.

Captain Haworth only had about 50 men with him and now, joined by Major Frankland and Captain H. M. Farmar, Brigade Staff Captain, found themselves under the cliffs on the right of the beach and began to work their way towards the ruined lighthouse.

The ground at the southern end of this Peninsula was undulating and very confusing to someone there for the first time. Also the maps available, apart from being inaccurate, were by now rather soggy.

The British map showed the high ground above Cape Helles as culminating in a single mound, marked Hill 138, due north of the lighthouse, and Brigadier General Hare's orders had only mentioned the redoubt on Hill 138. This was very misleading. There was in fact a second and higher crest some 400 yards to the south east of Hill 138, (known as Guezji Baba on which the Helles Memorial is now built) also holding a redoubt, being larger than its companion on Hill 138. These redoubts were later referred to as No.1 and No.2.

When Captain Haworth and A Company, still with Major Frankland, reached the top of the cliff north west of the old lighthouse they immediately came under fire from the larger of the two redoubts. For some time the smaller redoubt seems to have been ignored.

Captain Shaw and the remainder of B Company made an independent attack on Hill 138, but they were held up by wire on the forward slopes.. This was after errors in identifying some of the high features in the immediate area i.e.Hill 138, Guezji Baba and Hill 141, and this caused a great deal of confusion. At the end of this day Captain Shaw found himself with only 110 men out of an original strength of 205. He himself was killed in action on 4 June 1915, in the Third Battle of Krithia. As he has no known grave, his name is recorded on the Helles Memorial.

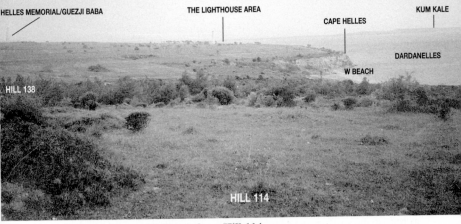

HELLES MEMORIAL/GUEZJI BABA   THE LIGHTHOUSE AREA   KUM KALE
CAPE HELLES
DARDANELLES
W BEACH
HILL 138
HILL 114

Looking towards W Beach from Hill 114.

However, despite these two attacks, by 8.30 am it soon became clear that no general concerted effort was possible, only a case of small parties making independent attacks. It was at this time that Major Frankland was killed whilst carrying out a reconnaissance beyond the lighthouse in the direction of V Beach, so Captain Farmar took over his duties.

It has to be remembered that the covering force was still without anyone to command it, and at this stage there was no one to control and co-ordinate operations on the beach.

By now Captain Willis and Major Adams, with C and D Companies respectively, were fighting grimly towards the summit of Hill 114, desperately trying to join up with one and a half companies of the Royal Fusiliers who were slowly advancing from X Beach.

On W Beach itself, which had now been secured, but at a terrible price, preparations were being made for the disembarkation of the main body by the Principal Beach Master, Captain Phillimore RN and the Principal Military Landing Officer, Brigadier General Roper and their staffs. Members of 1/2 London Field Company began the construction of exits from the beach whilst three platoons of the Anson Battalion (of the Royal Naval Division), who were due to assist in bringing supplies ashore that day, were pushed into the line to assist because the 1/LF were so short of men.

The original plan was that the 1/LF would not be reinforced as W beach was considered to be better protected from the Turkish guns on the Asiatic shore than V Beach. However, Lieutenant General Hunter-Weston, on board HMS *Euryalus,* 1000 yards offshore, had been given misleading reports regarding the apparent success at V Beach; and having realised that the 1/LF at W Beach required assistance, he diverted 1/Essex Regiment to them.

With their Commanding Officer, Lieutenant Colonel Owen Godfrey Faussett DSO, the 1/Essex had left the UK 1,000 strong, 'magnificent men, tall, well-built and trained to the moment'. W and X Companies transferred from the transport ship *Dongola* to a minesweeper and then to small boats for the landing, which took place at about 9.00 am.

Also at about 9.00am Brigadier General Napier and his 88 Brigade Staff, including his brigade major, Captain J.H.D. Costeker, Major Carr and his two platoons from W Coy, 4/Worcester Regiment, together with two companies 2/Hampshire Regiment, had embarked from their transport *Aragon* to a minesweeper and then to small boats, which were towed towards the SS *River Clyde*. These had already been used by 1/RDF and 'were much damaged by fire and blood mixed with seawater ran over the boots of the troops as they sat packed in the laden boats'. They had had to sit and watch the inferno on V Beach and then found it impossible to land when the floating bridge of lighters swung away from the beach and left a great gap. Many men had been killed and Major Carr, leaving Brigadier General Napier and his Staff to their own devices, collected his remnants together and took shelter on the collier, where he remained all day.

Later, at 10.21 am that morning, General Hamilton, now realising the difficulties at V Beach, diverted the remainder of the Main Force to W Beach. This was made up of the balance of 88 Brigade, with Brigadier General Henry Napier, and included the 2/Hampshires, 5/Royal Scots and the balance of the 4/Worcesters,

An army chaplain arriving at W Beach described the scene:

100 corpses laying in rows on the sand unrecognisable, their drenched bloodstained uniforms drying in the sun...the wounded lay all over the beach, on ledges of rock, wherever they could get any shelter. Some lay dead half way up the cliff holding a rifle in their hands.

By about 10.00 am all of 1/Essex were ashore, but there were no senior officer to give them any orders. Colonel Godfrey Faussett therefore ordered an advance of his men, some to assist 1/LF on Hill 114, who were soon adapting the Turkish trenches ready for any counter attack. Lieutenant Ward, the Company Commander of W Company, was killed at this time. X Company 1/Essex clambered up the cliff on the right hand side of the beach to connect up with 2/RF from X Beach with a view to assisting Captain Shaw and his Lancashire Fusiliers, pinned down on Hill 138.

Lt Col O G Godfrey
Faussett DSO
4/Worcestershire
Regiment

Captain G M Paxton MC and 1/Essex Regiment – survivors in 1918 after having landed on Gallipoli, April 1915.

By 11.30 am the summit of Hill 114 had been reinforced by C and D Companies 1/LF along with elements from 2/Hampshires and 1/Essex, all to support 2/RF from X Beach who had arrived there about 11.00am.

The loss of experienced senior officers was now telling on the landings at both W and V beaches. Some confusion and uncertainly reigned as no orders were given. Eventually, late that morning, Captain Bolton, a GHQ Liaison Officer, sent a signal to the 29th Division:

> *Send someone ashore to order advance. No brigade HQ here and no divisional staff. Still hung up as nothing has come ashore for hour and half.*

Following this Colonel Wolley Dod, the Division's senior operations staff officer (GS01), landed at 12.30 pm, after which some semblance of order was established. In a telegram to HQ at 1.22pm he confirmed his decision to send the 4/Worcesters, now arriving at W Beach, to attack Hill 138.

Map denotes situation of 1/Essex Regiment on morning of 25 April.
Essex Regimental Museum, Chelmsford

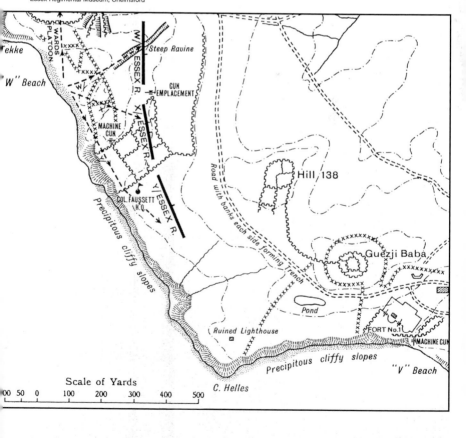

1/Essex Regiment landing on W Beach. Note dead bodies lying in the water, and the *Queen Lizzie* just behind Tekke Burnu.

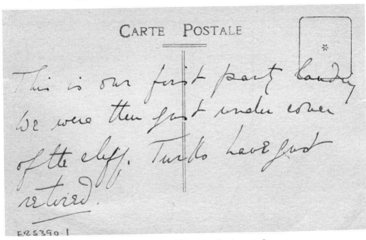

Written on the back of the above 1/Essex photograph. Essex Regimental Museum

It should be mentioned here that Captain Farmer, acting brigade major, had sent a message to W Beach at 12.25 pm strongly suggesting that troop landings would be a lot easier opposite the lighthouse. However this was not seen by Colonel Wolley-Dod until the majority of the 4/Worcesters had actually landed. On W Beach, too late for action.

Meantime Captain Haworth and A Company 1/LF lay out near the

TEKKE BURNU
(CAPE TEKKE)

REMAINS OF TRENCHES

SITE OF
'PORT TALBOT'
HARBOUR

1/ESSEX

W Beach today, looking west – little changed since 1/Essex landed on 25 April 1915.

old lighthouse, some 100 yards from the cliff edge, heads down, held up by rifle fire and rows of barbed wire. They had succeeded in cutting some of the wire, but heavy enemy fire held up any advance.

Now it was some time before 4/Worcesters drew up their plan to attack Hill 138 It was realised that paths must be cut through the wire entanglements in order to capture Hill 138 so, led by Captain Ray, volunteers from 4/Worcesters, used the only tools available – hand wire cutters – to carry out their dangerous task, all under intense fire. Despite casualties, lanes were cut, and at about 2.15 pm the troops were able to move forward and at 3.00 pm, both the 4/Worcesters and the 1/Essex successfully overran Hill 138, where Colonel Godfrey Faussett, 1/Essex, immediately established his Headquarters. (The Colonel was to lose his life six days later and is buried in Redoubt Cemetery.) These troops were then able to reinforce the beleaguered Lancashire Fusiliers. An attempt was made to advance eastwards but was held up by more uncut barbed wire and rifle and machine fire from Guezji Baba, some 300 yards away. It was during these attempts to break out that Captain Ray was killed. There were so many gallant individual efforts of continuous courage by the wire cutters that day before the job was eventually done.

At the cost of many brave lives, lanes were cut in the wire and it became possible for attacking troops to dash through the gaps.
An eye witness recalls:

Is that a charge?..what I see is crouching figures, some almost bent double, others jogtrotting over the grass with bright sun rays flashing on their bayonets. Now and again a figure falls and lies still – very still – in a crumpled heap: and all the time

4/Worcesters using wirecutters under fire at Cape Helles.
(Worcestershire Regiment Museum)

the crack crack of musketry and the pop-popping of machine guns never cease.

At last 4/Worcesters captured Guezji Baba and began to reverse the trenches on the cliff top and bury their dead comrades. However Colonel Wolley Dod received a message at 5.00 pm that the landing at V Beach had been seriously held up and the situation required urgent

Map denotes situation at nightfall 25 April 1915. Essex Regimental Museum, Chelmsford

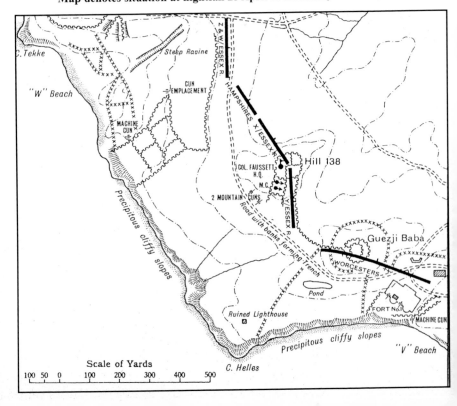

assistance. A rapid advance from W Beach was now essential in order to clear the Turkish trenches on the western flank of V Beach. 4/Worcesters were therefore ordered to attack the edge of the cliff above V Beach but were met with stubborn fire from the Turks and were not able to advance. Colonel Wolley Dod played a pivotal role throughout this chaotic day in endeavouring to maintain some sort of order and momentum and the War Diary of the 29th Division refers to his involvement frequently.

By now darkness was closing in. Little had changed since late afternoon and so it was therefore decided to consolidate the ground gained, to bring in the scattered men of various companies, and to prepare to face the inevitable counter-attack that night. A line was then established by the men of 4/Worcesters, 1/Essex and 2/Hampshires, reaching from the ruins of Fort No. 1 just above V Beach through Guezji Baba, Hill 138 and north of Hill 114 to X Beach.
Colonel Cayley, 1/Essex, wrote:

> *By this time it was evening and we dug in... By the time my right company reached the demolished fort just short of the cliff above V Beach we could look down on the beach from one point.*
> *It was an awesome sight – simply rows of dead men.*

It had become apparent about midday that a terrible inertia had seized the 2,000 men on the heights above W Beach. Tired, shaken by the fierce resistance of the enemy, shocked by the heavy losses amongst their officers, the men were overwrought from the tension of the landing and matters were made much worse by the loss of their commander, Brigadier-General Hare O.C. Covering Force. It had been a day of gallantry, heroism, self sacrifice and courage born of desperation.

Repositioned new lighthouse on Cape Helles.

APPROXIMATE POSITION OF
WIRE CUT BY 4/WORCESTERS

It had not been perhaps fully realised that the landing in open boats would not be the most difficult task. Pressing forward into unknown territory with scattered units was proving equally difficult and for some of the time there was physically no one on shore to initiate a fresh plan with clear and definite orders. The idea of a united advance to Achi Baba, the main objective of the day, over 750 feet high and some four miles distant, which dominated the surrounding countryside and glowered like some maleovolent god on the events below, fell to pieces when so little progress could be made from the beaches. Such a pity, when the Allies heavily outnumbered the enemy.

It must not be forgotten, either, that the men of the 29th Division for the most part had faced their first terrifying experience of modern warfare. They were worn out and at nightfall were in some disarray. The great number of casualties suffered in the landing had not been anticipated and few arrangements had been made to deal with them. W Beach was an appalling place to be when facilities were so rudimentary.

A medical orderly wrote:

It was difficult to select the most urgent cases. Men had lost arms and legs, brains oozed out of shattered skulls, and lungs protruded from riven chests; many had lost their faces, and were, I should think, unrecognisable to their friends. One poor chap had lost his nose and most of his face, and we were obliged to take off an arm, the other hand and extract two bullets like shark's teeth from his thigh, besides minor operations. It was really a precious hour or more wasted, for I saw him the next morning being carried to the mortuary.

Less than half of the 1/LF had won through that day.

The strength of the Battalion at the landing was 25 officers and 918 men. On 26 April their Battalion strength was 15 officers and 411 other ranks The remainder were either killed, wounded or missing, a total of 517 casualties or 55%. However, their actions were to become legend. W Beach became known as Lancashire Landing out of profound respect for what those men had achieved that day. The Lancashire Fusiliers, at the end of the Campaign, left behind 1,816 men on the Gallipoli Peninsula and have the most names on the Helles Memorial to the Missing, a total of 1,329.

In *Gallipoli* John Masefield concluded:

Our men achieved a feat without parallel in war, and no other troops in the world...would have made good those beaches on the 25th of April.

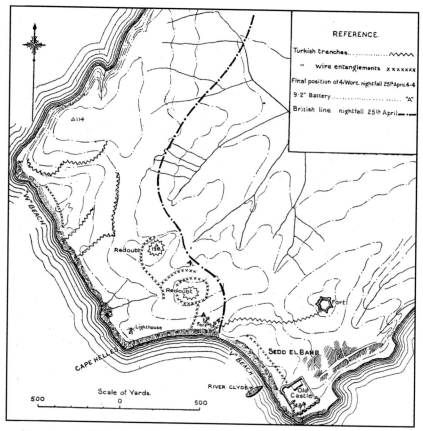

Situation of 4/Worcestershire Regiment at the end of 25 April, 1915.
Worcestershire Regiment Museum

Sincere tributes were made to the gallantry and fighting qualities of 1/LF which included one by General Hamilton and also one from HMS *Euryalus* which read:

> We are as proud as can be to have had the honour to carry your splendid Regiment. We feel for you all in your great losses as if it were our own ship's company, but know the magnificent gallantry of your regiment has made the name more famous than ever.

26 and 27 April

A strong defensive position had been formed on the line held at the end of 25 April, and the next morning the first meal was eaten. An officer of 1/Essex wrote:

> You should have seen us, unshaven, filthy and begrimed, fairly ramming down bully beef and biscuits and drinking tea out of a canteen.

Despite constant sniping throughout the following two days, units were re-organised, with the some of 88 Brigade reforming at Hill 138 on April 27, ready for the advance on Krithia.

On the 26th 4/Worcesters, at 2.30pm assisted in the attack on Hill 141, which was taken at last.

25 April 1915 was a day that abounded with countless examples of immense courage, stoic fortitude, fearless resolve and great gallantry. Six Victoria Crosses were eventually awarded to men of the 1/Lancashire Fusiliers for actions during the landings at W Beach that day, almost equalling the seven VCs before breakfast awarded to the men of the 24th Foot at Rorke's Drift, South Africa, in January 1879.

That followed an unusual (but not unprecedented) decision by the military to ask the survivors of the action on W Beach to elect six recipients of the award because it was felt that the Regiment comprised 'equally brave and distinguished people'.

On 15 May Major General Sir Aylmer Hunter-Weston (GOC 29th Division) wrote:

> The landing is a deed of heroism that has seldom been equalled and I strongly recommend that the gallantry of the deed may be recognised by the bestowal of six VCs on the two most distinguished officers and the four most distinguished NCOs and men, namely Captains C Bromley and R R Willis, Sergeants A. Richards and F E Stubbs, Corporal Grimshaw and Private W. Keneally.

Sir Ian Hamilton happily endorsed these recommendations but for some months uncertainty and confusion reigned at the War Office regarding the rules governing the award of the Victoria Cross. The whole matter then became somewhat unsatisfactory in that only three VCs were awarded in August 1915, those going to Captain Willis selected by the officers, Sergeant Richards selected by the NCOs and Private Keneally selected by the other ranks.

The London Gazette on 24 August 1915 announced:

> The King has been pleased to award the Victoria Cross to the undermentioned officers, non-commissioned officers, and men in recognition of their most conspicuous bravery and devotion to duty in the field:
>
> Captain Richard Raymond Willis
>
> No 1293 Sergeant Alfred Richards
>
> No 1809 Private William Keneally, all of 1/Lancashire Fusiliers.

Other awards followed, including a DSO to Captain Haworth and the DCM to Corporal Grimshaw

However Captain Bromley, Sergeant Stubbs and Corporal Grimshaw had been excluded from receiving the ultimate award despite being elected by their surviving colleagues. It was only due to the persistent efforts of the now Brigadier General Owen Wolley-Dod, a Lancashire Fusilier himself and who, it will be recalled, landed on W Beach soon after midday on 25 April, that the case was re-examined. Finally in March 1917 the *London Gazette* belatedly announced the award of the Victoria Cross to these three men.

This was the only collective award of the Victoria Cross made in the First World War.

Captain Richard Willis

Born in Woking, Surrey on 19 October 1876, Richard Willis was educated at Harrow and the RMC Sandhurst. He spent his entire service career in the Lancashire Fusiliers, from 20 February 1897 to 26 November 1920, serving in India, Omdurman, Crete, Malta, Gibraltar and Egypt. He was a keen sportsman and an excellent shot. By 1915, Willis had commanded C Company for fifteen consecutive years, a somewhat unusual distinction. A famous painting by an *Illustrated London News* artist reputedly depicts Willis as its central figure, shouting encouragement to his men and holding a walking stick aloft which earned him the nickname *'Walking stick Willis'*.

Captain R R Willis,
1/Lancashire Fusiliers.

He faced both financial and health difficulties in later life. At the great age of 90, a widower, almost blind and very frail, he died in 1966 in a Cheltenham Nursing Home known as Faithful House.

Lieutenant Commander Arthur Coxon, whose father served with 5th Battalion Norfolk Regiment (*The Vanished Battalion* and the subject of a BBC documentary and a film *All the King's Men,* starring David Jason) and who was taken prisoner by the Turks at Azmak in August 1915, recalls being taught by Captain Willis at Nautical College Pangbourne, and remembers him as a rather sad and morose person whose class only saw him during history lessons. The College felt that Major Willis was perhaps the most remarkable member of their Staff, who could certainly entertain the cadets but who had little idea of teaching history!

Sergeant Alfred Richards

Alfred was born on 21 June 1879 in Plymouth, Devon. At the tender

Sgt A Richards
1/Lancashire Fusiliers.

age of 16 he became a band boy in the Regiment. He served with the 1/LF in Ireland, became a drummer and then travelled to Gibraltar, Malta, Crete and Alexandria. It was a good life and he excelled at football. As a lance corporal in 1907, he took his discharge when the Battalion returned to England, but after two months decided civilian life was not for him and re-enlisted, being sent to India.

At the landing on W Beach he was serving with C Company as a sergeant and endured agonies that day. Captain Willis saw him trying to get through the wire on the beach to some sort of cover with his leg 'horribly twisted'. His leg had been almost severed by machine gun fire, but as he knew that to stay on the beach behind the wire would be suicide, he told his men to follow him. Crawling through the wire in considerable pain, he dragged his lacerated leg behind him, yelling encouragement to his men as they advanced towards the Turks.

He suffered terribly and eventually had to have the leg amputated. Discharged from the Army in July 1915, after serving some twenty years with the Lancashire Fusiliers, he was awarded the Long Service and Good Conduct Medal. When he was told of the award of the VC, he said honestly that he did not remember much about the actual landing. This can be hardly surprising, considering the agony he must have been in.

He survived the Second World War in which he served with the Home Guard and died in Southfields, London, on 21 May 1953, after a short illness, at the age of seventy three. Survivors of the landings at Gallipoli were present at his funeral, and he was buried in Putney Vale Cemetery. In 1967, when the grave was reported to be in a sad state of disrepair, the trustees of the Lancashire Fusiliers paid for a new headstone with the regimental crest and inscription. His medals are in private hands.

Lance Sergeant William Keneally

William Keneally was from Wexford, Ireland, born on 26 December 1886. At 13, he worked down the mines as a pit boy until he decided to become a soldier like his father. All his service life was spent with 1/LF. W Beach proved to be his first

Pte W Keneally
1/Lanchashire Fusiliers.

experience of battle and an unforgettable one. He showed great determination as a runner after landing on the beach but then seeing his comrades suffering because they were held up on the barbed wire, decided to try and cut a way through. Despite facing almost certain death in the open, he made valiant efforts to create gaps but was unsuccessful. He was extremely fortunate to survive these actions. Having survived the landings, he then took part in the three battles for Krithia, but on 28 June, when the Battalion was commanded by Major Bromley, he was seriously wounded in Gully Ravine, and died the following day. He is buried in Lancashire Landing Cemetery (Plot C.104). (The different spelling of his name will be noted.)

Captain Cuthbert Bromley

His citation concluded:

Amongst the very many gallant officers and men engaged in this most hazardous undertaking, Major Bromley, Sergeant Stubbs and Sergeant Grimshaw have been selected by their comrades as having performed the most signal acts of bravery and devotion to duty.

Captain Bromley 1/Lancashire fusiliers.

Captain Cuthbert Bromley was Adjutant of the 1/LF and was born at Sutton Corner, Seaford, Sussex in September 1878. At school in Barnes he was a strong young man, a great sportsman, a keen athlete and could row well. A report in a contemporary newspaper contained the following remarks:

It was the wonderful spirit fostered by Bromley during years of camaraderie and fine example in the regiment which brought success at Cape Helles on the early morning of 25 April, 1915. His personal influence was immeasurable. He had made the Lancashire Fusiliers the champions in all India in military training, boxing, football and cross country running.

Those men who followed him ashore under hellish fire had true discipline. Bromley was with the men a leader and a comrade.

Reference has already been made to his energetic leadership just after the landing. Three days later, the Brigade Major led an attack on a small fir wood during the first advance on Krithia, and Captain Bromley was there. He was wounded in the knee afterwards, during a reconnaissance. Sergeant Burtchell carried him back to his lines to have the wound dressed. It was only then that the medical orderlies discovered that he had had a bullet in his back since 25 April, which he had not mentioned to anyone except those who had bandaged him up.

Sutton Corner Seaford birthplace of Captain C Bromley VC .

On his return from this treatment, he heard that his men had been in action at Krithia on 4 June and had suffered considerable loss. On 28 June a major attack in Gully Ravine took place, and C and D Company 1/LF were ordered to make a frontal attack in the area east of Fusilier Bluff. Newly promoted, Major Cuthbert Bromley led the charge, delivering in his inimitable way a rousing speech to his men before the whistle blew.

As he climbed over the parapet, he was hit in the foot. Determined not to leave the scene he grabbed two Turkish

Seaford War memorial where Bromley is commemorated.

rifles and tried to use them as crutches for a time. He ordered two young stretcher bears to carry him as he continued to direct the attack. However, this wound was serious, and he was ordered to Alexandria for treatment in the hospital there.

It was not possible to keep him away for long, and as soon as he could hobble he pleaded to be allowed to rejoin his Battalion. The transport ship *Royal Edward* was soon on its way back to the Peninsula, with Major Bromley on board. An enemy submarine, UB-14, spotted the ship and fired several torpedoes. Some found their mark and it was not long before the ship began to sink very quickly. Major Bromley stayed on board and prepared to go down with the ship whilst any men remained unplaced in the boats. Being brought up by the often rough seas around Seaford, he was a very strong swimmer, and decided to take his chance. He drowned before he could be picked up. It was suspected that a piece of wreckage or one of the rescue boats hit him and caused his death. His body was not recovered and his record shows that he was lost at sea, along with 861 others. He has no known grave, and his name is recorded on the Helles Memorial to the Missing.

Sergeant Grimshaw spoke very warmly of his Officer:

> *His bravery was superb. He set an example which was unequalled by anyone. He was admired by everyone. I remember seeing him once in the Landing, and he was one of the first men to reach the top of the cliffs.*

Sergeant Frank Edward Stubbs

He was born in London in 1888, and enlisted with the Lancashire Fusiliers as a boy solider. He served with them in India. Stubbs was with Captain Willis and C Company and was endeavouring to reach Hill 114 when he was killed. There was a single tree on top of the hill and Stubbs had just managed to lead his section there before he was hit.

Sgt. F E Stubbs,
1/Lancashire Fusiliers.

Lance Corporal John Elisha Grimshaw

John Grimshaw, the only true Lancastrian amongst the six VCs, was born in Wigan in 1893 and worked for many years as a carpenter at a colliery in the Wigan coalfields. He enlisted in the Lancashire Fusiliers in 1912 and served with them in India. As a signaller with C Company on 25 April 1915 he showed great bravery, coolness and impressive leadership during the landing. It was his job to send messages by

Cpl. J G Grimshaw, 1/Lancashire Fusiliers

semaphore to the divisional command on board HMS *Euryalus* once the cliff above W Beach had been reached. He survived the Gallipoli campaign and had a private soldier's stoical attitude to his life, writing in the summer of 1915:

It's terrible, though, is war, and I think it's worse here in Gallipoli than anywhere, for it is simply hell and you don't know but that the next minute will be your last. But we have to go some time, and we might as well go fighting for our country

He was severely frostbitten in November during the appalling winter storms at Suvla. Recuperating in England, he received the award of his DCM together with a gold watch with the inscription:

Presented to Sergeant J E Grimshaw from the public of Abram and district as a mark of appreciation on his securing the DCM for conspicuous bravery at Cape Helles on April 25 1915.

But he was dumbfounded when he heard in 1916 that he had been awarded the Victoria Cross and it took some time to convince him that this was indeed the case.

Serving in France in 1916 he was commissioned in the field, and later became a lieutenant colonel during his service as an army recruiting officer in Cardiff. He finally retired in 1953 after forty one years exemplary service. John Grimshaw made a point of attending the annual Gallipoli Day parades in Bury until he became too unwell to travel. He died in July 1980.

Towards the end of the Campaign, Ernest Raymond wrote in his novel, *Tell England*, of the evocative impressions the Gallipoli Peninsula had made on him:

It would be a wonderful trip, skirting by daylight the coastline of the Peninsula, till we round the point and looked upon the Helles Beaches, the sacred site of the first and most marvellous battle of the Dardanelles campaign. It was a pilgrimage to a shrine that stretched before us on the morrow....

As I gazed from its side towards the Suvla that we were leaving, the whole line of the Peninsula came into panorama before me. The sun, just awake, bathed a long, waving skyline that rose at two point to dominant levels. One was Sari Bair, the stately hill which stood inviolate, although an army had dashed itself against its fastnesses. The other, lower down the skyline, was Achi Baba, as impregnable as her sister, Sari Bair. The story of the campaign was the story of these two hills.

For perfect charm, I recall no trip to equal this cruise betimes in the sparkling Aegean. .. I sprang my imagination to the alert position, that I might not miss one thrill, when we should enter the bay whose waters played on W Beach. Conceive it: there would meet my gaze a stretch of lapping water, a width of beach, and a bluff hill; and I must say: 'Here were confused battle, and blood filtering through the ground. There was agony here, and quivering flesh. Here the promises of straight limbs, keen eyes, and clear cheeks were cancelled in a spring morning...Hither a thousand destinies converged upon the beach, and here they closed.

In conclusion, perhaps the words of Rudyard Kipling form a fitting epitaph and reflect the steadfastness, stalwart courage and great gallantry in the most daunting circumstances of the landings at Helles on 25th April 1915.

All that they had they gave – they gave; and they shall not return,
For these are those that have no grave where any heart may mourn.

WALK NO 3: W BEACH

W BEACH: Sedd El Bahr 2 kms and 6.5 kms from Krithia.
Time allowed from Sedd El Bahr – 2 hours round trip. Eceabat is 31 kms from W Beach.

It should be mentioned, particularly as far as the area around W Beach is concerned, that most of the land is private property and care should be shown when exploring. There are no footpaths, just rough tracks, sheep and goats roam freely and the fields of crops should be respected and not trampled over. A cheery wave of the hand and a smile to the local shepherd or farmer is appreciated.

Happily the Turkish Government have now lifted the ban on visiting the military installations and the beach and it is possible to explore the whole area without restrictions.

From X Beach the coastal road south should be followed for about 1500 metres until on the bend in the road, not far from the summit of Hill 114, a rough track on the right hand side can be found. This was the original entrance to the Turkish garrison and derelict concrete bunkers, rusty barbed wire, a sentry's hut and other debris can be seen.

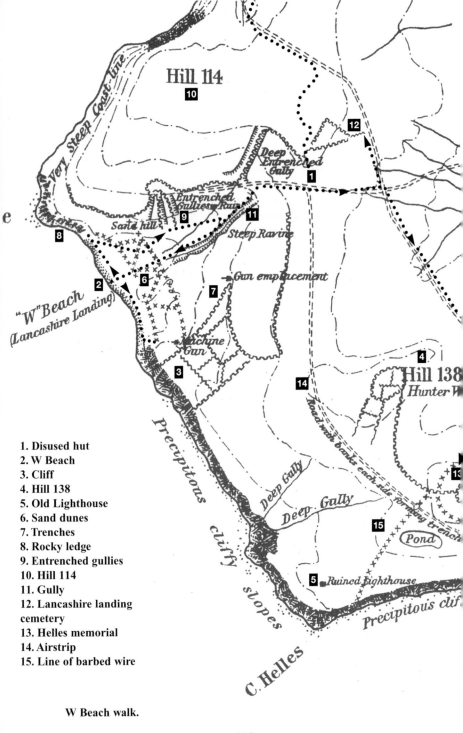

1. Disused hut
2. W Beach
3. Cliff
4. Hill 138
5. Old Lighthouse
6. Sand dunes
7. Trenches
8. Rocky ledge
9. Entrenched gullies
10. Hill 114
11. Gully
12. Lancashire landing cemetery
13. Helles memorial
14. Airstrip
15. Line of barbed wire

W Beach walk.

Follow the track as it winds downhill until you reach a **disused hut (1)**. Turn right and walk down the gully lined with trees and shrubs for about 500 metres until you reach the wind-blown sand dunes and the sandy track **to W Beach (2)** itself.

W Beach retains its special character just because access has been so limited and is little changed. Unlike the area of V Beach, there are no modern houses, mosques, or cafes to intrude on one's thoughts. The same steep yellow cliffs enclose the white sand beach on either side, and in the centre can be seen the remains of old trenches, now covered in low scrub, interspersed with a few young pines.

Apart from freely walking along the beach, noting the rusting remains of the piers which still jut out into the shallow water, together with wrecks of old lighters, and the chunks of rusty metal on the beach, it is perhaps salutary to stand facing out to sea and try and imagine that heroic landing so many years ago. If one then turns and then stands with one's back to the water, it is possible to plot the Turkish defences put so carefully in place that it had become a death trap.

On the right is the **cliff (3)** up which Captain Haworth and some of A Company clambered. With its interlinking trenches on top and two machine gun emplacements, the first just 100 yards from the cliff top whilst the other was a further 200 yards inland, it proved a hard task. Beyond this cliff, surrounded by further trenches, was the objective of the redoubt on **Hill 138 (4)**, about 600 yards away, later to be known as Hunter Weston Hill when VIII Corps established its headquarters in dugouts on its slopes.

It was from the top of this cliff that Captain Haworth and his men, together with Major Frankland went forward towards the **old lighthouse (5)** for some 6-700 yards beyond which Major Frankland was killed. It is not possible to see the site of the ruined lighthouse from the beach and the present day lighthouse is in a slightly different position.

In the **centre of the beach (6)** one can see the sand dunes with tussocks of rough grass. Just in front of you were two main lines of barbed wire, with inter connecting diagonal rows in support, all at least three feet in height. The wire began almost at the water's edge, had a depth of about 100 yards and ran virtually the whole length of the bay. It was a terrifying obstacle in itself, and one which caused appalling casualties. The trip wires and mines had been put in the sea, with further land mines actually on the beach.

It is here one can recall the agony and courage of that morning, when six very ordinary men were deemed by their colleagues to have carried out some extraordinary acts of valour and recall Captain Shaw's words,

> *a whole line in a row at the edge of the sands. The sea behind was absolutely crimson, and you could hear the groans through the rattle of musketry.*

If one walks into the sand dunes with care it is possible to follow some of the **trench lines (7)** just above the centre. Although difficult to see after years of blowing sand and encroaching scrub, battlefield debris can still be uncovered, a broken rum jar here, a rusty bucket there, a

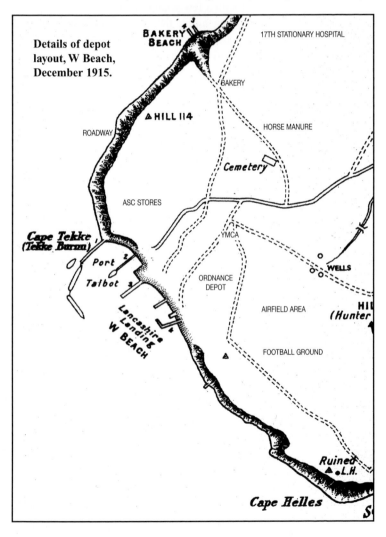

Details of depot layout, W Beach, December 1915.

spent round – all adding to the evocation of those momentous days.

The **rocky ledge at the base of the steep cliff on the left (8)** was where Brigadier General Hare and Major Frankland landed. The present day concrete structure has nothing to do with the Gallipoli campaign. From here an advance was made up the cliff to the main Turkish defensive position, which was thirty yards away. Captain Cuthbert Bromley played his part that morning and personally encouraged and led small groups of men to the top. Walk a short way inland along the track. It is possible to clamber up the side of the short but **steep gullies (9)** on the left, which had originally been entrenched, to the top of the cliff, leading up to Hill 114. The remains of shallow trenches will be seen, some could be British. There are fine views from the top of the cliff – of the remains of the four piers, Hill 138 and

W Beach became the main British camp at Helles.

the Helles Memorial. Whilst there are no paths it is possible to walk towards the summit of **Hill 114 (10)** following the route of Captain Willis and Major Adams with C and D Companies, where they finally linked up with a small force of 1/RF from X Beach at the end of the morning. Two 30,000 gallon concrete reservoirs can be found built during the summer of 1915 by the Royal Monmouth Royal Engineers, with each being capable of holding three days supply of drinking water. An inscription can be seen which reads '5 COY MON RE AUG 1915'.

Before leaving the vicinity of W Beach it is worth recalling that this area became the main British camp at Helles after the landings, with a breakwater being formed to protect the piers used for landing supplies from bad seas and heavy swells.

A roadway was built by Egyptian labourers and some Turkish prisoners which eventually linked Gully Beach with Lancashire Landing and was in constant use by a real cross section of 'promenaders', as Compton Macenzie recalled.

The beach became an 'ant's nest in revolution', according to Sir Ian Hamilton, and the main supply dump of rations, water, weapons, ammunition, transport including horses, together with field hospitals and kitchens. A telegraph office was linked by submarine cable with Limnos (Lemnos) Anzac and Imbros. Troops were also known to take a short swim as a welcome moment of relaxation – and getting clean! It was the main evacuation area for the British in January 1916.

Return to the main coastal road by **walking up the gully (11)** for about 500 metres to the rough track. You will be walking in the direction of the British advance on 25 April, once the cliffs and the beach had been secured and the troops able to slowly make their way to the flatter ground. On reaching the track, turn right. After a few hundred metres, this eventually joins up with the tarmac road. Turn sharp left and after a short distance you will arrive at **Lancashire Landing Cemetery (12)**, on the eastern slope of Hill 114.

Lancashire Landing Cemetery

Begun immediately after the landings, and overlooking W Beach, it is named after the beach on which the Lancashire Fusiliers landed. Out of the 1253 graves, Row I contains the graves of 86 men of 1/Lancashire Fusiliers, 82 of them unknown. Captain Thomas Bowyer-Lane Maunsell will be found in Plot I:100, and Lance Sergeant William Keneally VC's grave can be seen in Plot C 104. He was killed on 29 June during the Battle of Gully Ravine. In April and May, with its irises in full bloom, it is one of the loveliest cemeteries on the Peninsula.

Original burials in Lancashire Landing cemetery, Helles.

On leaving the Cemetery, if you stand with your back to the gateway, with its evocative plaque, to your front you will clearly see the **Helles Memorial (13)** built on the site of the redoubt, Guezji Baba.

Lancashire Landing Cemetery today.

Just to the right of the Memorial is the modern lighthouse, and little further right, the area of W Beach. On a good day if you look into the distance on your left, you should see Achi Baba on the horizon. Leave the cemetery and continue in the direction of Sedd El Bahr. After some 600 metres you will pass over **Hill 138 (4)** and see the **Helles Memorial site (13)**, some 400 metres on the right. This direction is parallel with the position secured by the 1/Essex Regiment, the 1/Hampshire Regiment and 4/Worcestershire Regiment by the evening of 25 April 1915. During the night these weary British troops had to face several fierce counter attacks by the Turks along the whole line from close to X Beach to Guezji Baba. Somehow or other these attacks were repelled and the ground held.

In this vicinity too, on the flatter ground, Commander Charles Samson endeavoured to maintain a **small emergency RNAS airstrip(14)**, although no evidence exists today. The innovative Commander Samson had already made a 800 metre airstrip on Tenedos, using oil drums filled with concrete to flatten a vineyard, but soon realised that Tenedos was too far away for aircraft to cover the entire Peninsula, it being about 18 miles from Helles. Whilst the Lancashire Landing airstrip proved useful, mainly for observation, it was eventually moved to Imbros, with the French taking over the Tenedos airstrip.

Turning right, continue to the tall white monument of the **Helles Memorial to the Missing (13)**, almost stark in its simplicity, where there is a car park.

Whilst the main purpose is to visit the Memorial and study the panels inscribed with the names of the Missing of the Gallipoli Campaign, it is worth standing on the top of the steps with your back to the Memorial facing the sea and imagine **the huge barricade of barbed wire (15)** which ran for about 500 metres from here, the site of Guezji Baba, due south to the cliffs of Cape Helles in the direction of the present day lighthouse. This was the wire that caused such difficulty for the British troops who tried to move from W Beach to link up and assist their comrades trapped on V Beach. Both the 1/Essex Regiment and 4/Worcester Regiment, together with the sad remnants of 1/Lancashire Fusiliers, eventually broke their way through the wire to capture Guezji Baba by mid-afternoon on 25 April. W Beach is on your right, V Beach and Morto Bay on your left. The close proximity of these three main beaches brings home the fact that the landings were a concerted effort with a main objective, and not separate actions unconnected with each other. Achi Baba is a good four miles behind you to the north.

Helles Memorial to the Missing

Situated as it is overlooking the Dardanelles towards ancient city of Troy, the Helles Memorial is both the Memorial to the Gallipoli Campaign and to the 20,763 men who fell in that campaign and whose bodies were never found, or who were lost or buried at sea in Gallipoli waters. Inscribed on it are the names of all the ships that took part in the campaign and the titles of the army formations and units which served on the Peninsula together with the names of 18,985 sailors, soldiers and marines from the United Kingdom, 248 soldiers from Australia and 1,530 soldiers of the Indian Army.

No visit to the Gallipoli Peninsula would be complete without paying one's respects at this simple and somewhat austere monument. The British Ceremony held here on the morning of 25 April each year is usually understated and low key, with perhaps a hundred or so attending.

Completed in 1924, the cenotaph is almost 33 metres high. On each of its four sides are large tablets listing the units who served. On the surrounding walls (both inside and out) are large panels where the names of officers and men who fell and who have no known grave and includes those who were buried at sea and the names of vessels involved in the Campaign. Four recipients of the Victoria Cross are listed, three of whose names will be very familiar – Sub Lieutenant A

Helles Memorial to the Missing.

Tisdall, (Panel 8) Captain C. Bromley (Panel 218) and Sergeant F. Stubbs (Panel 59). The last is Captain G. O'Sullivan, 1/Royal Inniskilling Fusiliers (Panel 97).

This marks the conclusion of the walk in the W Beach area. It is simple to return to your starting point. However, it is also practical to continue your journey and visit V Beach.

W Beach, after the landings. Note the piers, whose rusty remains and the remains of ships hulls can still be seen today.

Chapter Five

V BEACH
Carnage and courage

On scorching days in summer at the southern most tip of the Gallipoli Peninsula the local villagers of Sedd El Bahr can be found splashing in the sea, children shrieking, laughing and playing on the sandy beach, whilst their grandfathers enjoy a cool drink and a game of backgammon in the nearby shady taverna.

But on a balmy early spring day it is still possible to walk completely alone along the beach, kneel down by a long low sandy bank and gaze out to sea, quietly reflecting on the momentous event that took place here those long years ago. The stony pier, whilst smaller, still exists, and whilst it is not difficult to imagine the huge shape of the collier *SS River Clyde* rammed against it, not so the

V Beach map showing Turkish defences and position of *SS River Clyde*.

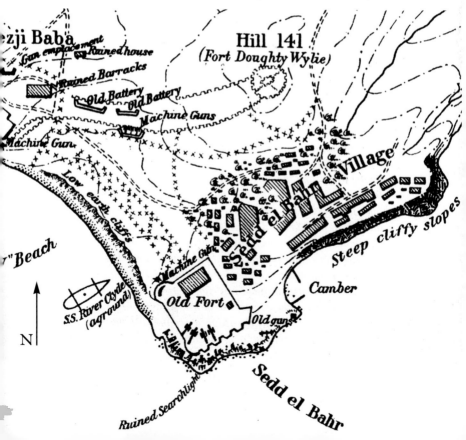

LT. COL DOUGHTY-WYLIE'S GRAVE

HILL 141

Panoramic view of V Beach area.

terrifying sound of withering machine gun as it swept through the ranks of the men of the 29th Division on 25 April 1915.

V beach is one mile south of W Beach, and forms a natural amphitheatre, which rises to about one hundred feet. It is dominated on the west by Fort No. 1 and on the east by the Old Fort (also known as Fort No. 3) and the village of Sedd El Bahr. Beyond the village was a castle on Hill 141. The beach was ten yards wide and three hundred yards long with a four to five foot sand bank stretching almost the length of the beach. The shelter this bank could afford to exposed troops was to prove invaluable during the thirty-two hours that ensued after the landings.

In his despatch of May 20 1915, General Sir Ian Hamilton described some of the obstacles that had to be overcome.

At the south east extremity of the beach, between the shore and the village, stands the old fort of Sedd El Bahr, a battered ruin with wide breaches in its walls and mounds of fallen masonry within and around it. On the ridge to the North, overlooking the amphitheatre, stands a ruined barrack. Both of these buildings, as well as Fort No. 1, had been long bombarded by the Fleet, and the guns of the fort had been put out of action; but their crumbled walls and the ruined outskirts of the village afforded cover for riflemen, while from the terraced slopes already described the defenders were able to command the open beach, as a stage is overlooked from the balconies of a theatre. On the very margin of the beach a strong barbed wire entanglement, made of a heavier material and longer barbs that I have ever seen elsewhere, ran right across from the old fort of Sedd El Bahr to the foot of the north-western headland. Two-thirds of the way up to the ridge a second and even stronger entanglement crossed the amphitheatre, passing in front of the

SEDD EL BAHR — OLD FORT — SS RIVER CLYDE BEACHED — V BEACH — V BEACH CEMETERY — FORT NO 1

old barrack and ending in the outskirts of the village. A third transverse entanglement, joining these two, ran up the hill near the eastern end of the beach, and almost at right angles to it. Above the upper entanglement the ground was scored with the enemy's trenches, in one of which four pom-poms were emplaced; in others were dummy pom-poms to draw fire, while the debris of the shattered buildings on either flank afforded cover and concealment for a number of machine-guns, which brought a cross fire to bear on the ground already swept by rifle fire from the ridge.

As mentioned the Old Fort of Sedd El Bahr, together with Fort No. 1 and the castle/old barracks building, on the summit of Hill 141, had been bombarded heavily by the fleet. It is clear that whilst the guns at the forts could no longer fire, the damaged ruins and rubble of the old fort and the remains of the village outskirts still provided good cover for Turkish rifles.

Sedd-El-Bahr fort, photographed after its capture. Maxim guns had been placed in the ports and gaps in the wall and on the slope of the cliff.

V Beach and Sedd El Bahr village.

It can be seen from the sketch made by Captain Geddes on the morning of 25 April that V Beach was like a stage, overlooked by forts No.1 and 3 and some narrow trenches. A significant factor was that these trenches, well hidden and marked clearly on the sketch, had not been destroyed beforehand. They were so well disguised that not even the officers of the *SS River Clyde* were aware of these trenches until the afternoon of 25 April. Perhaps the fact that the Royal Navy fired a considerable number of armour piercing shells as opposed to shrapnel nullified the Allied bombardment.

The sketch also shows the strong barbed wire referred to by General Sir Ian Hamilton running across the beach from the old fort to the low cliff that jutted up on the west.

Sketch of V Beach 25 April, 1915, by Captain G W Geddes.

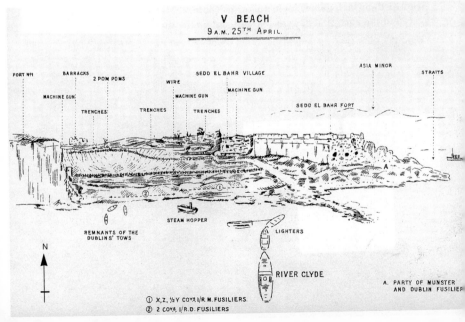

The Turks had reinforced this naturally strong position with a company of infantry from the 3/26 Regiment, together with pom-poms and four old pattern Maxim machine guns situated for maximum effect. (The Turks recorded in 1926 that two of these machine guns were knocked out by the Royal Navy before the landings occurred.)

As described in the **Grand Plan**, the task of the 29th Division was to attack the Kilid Bair Plateau from the south by landing at the beaches denoted:Y- X- W -V and S with the main objective of the day being a line from coast to coast running through Achi Baba (now known as Alcitepe).

The 29th Division

The famous 29th Division was the only regular Division involved in the Landings and was the most junior of the five improvised 'Old Army' Divisions. The men were all regular troops except some Territorial Force including the Royal Engineers, Royal Army Medical Corps, signallers, Army Service Corps and 1/5 Royal Scots.

Included in the artillery support was 'L' Battery, which in September 1914 became renowned for its stalwart efforts to hold up the German advance at Nery in the Retreat from Mons and where men of the Battery were awarded three Victoria Crosses for their bravery.

The initial landings would include 2000 men at Y Beach and a balance of 2900 men at X, W, V and S Beach beaches as well as the Camber. They would be followed by 2100 men from the SS *River Clyde* and 1200 men from the second line of tows. The 29th Division would form a Covering Force from its own 86 Brigade, along with some attached units, under Brigadier General Hare

The Gallipoli Campaign proved to be the birthplace of innovative ideas, makeshift solutions and rudimentary improvements to equipment, some more successful than others. One of the most remarkable was the conversion of a ten year old collier into a modern-day Trojan horse.

This innovative improvisation was an idea put forward by Commander Unwin, a 51 year old Boer War veteran and Merchant Navy officer, brought out of retirement in August 1914 and at this time Captain of HMS *Hussar*. He had been given the task of assisting in changing the peaceful, deep, natural harbour of Mudros into a naval base under the newly appointed Governor of Lemnos, Rear Admiral Wemyss. The SS *River Clyde* was an innocent looking ten year old collier built in Glasgow and used in the rather mundane task of transporting mules from North Africa. Whilst there was initial pessimism from the Staff that this scheme could work, Rear Admiral Wemyss was enthusiastic. Some important aspects which were considered were: there would be an important element of surprise because of the large number of troops landed; the troops would have more protection in the collier and V Beach was larger than the other beaches and would need more reinforcements quickly.

As it was known that there would be a shortage of boats available for ferrying the troops to the shore, using the collier would also mean that the landing of 2,000 reinforcements after the initial wave would double the number on shore within minutes.

The plan was eventually approved. Work started on 12 April. The conversion of the ship included cutting two wide openings, called sally ports, in each side of the hull, underneath which were hung specially made gangways extending to the bows. The men would emerge through the sally ports, run along broad gangplanks to a platform fixed up under the vessel's bows and on to a floating bridge between ship and shore, made up of a flat bottomed steam hopper, the *Argyll*, which would be towed towards Cape Helles by *SS River Clyde*. Commander Unwin, now OC the collier, had placed a junior officer, 20 year old Midshipman George Drewry, in command of the hopper, with a small Greek crew. The steam hopper would be set free just before beaching to form the bridge. As a contingency Unwin had also planned to tow three lighters specially adapted to fill in any gaps between the bows of the collier and the stern of the hopper.

Commander Edward Unwin RN.

Another innovation was the inclusion of armoured car units. These had first appeared in Antwerp alongside the

SS River Clyde **being prepared at Mudros harbour for the landing at V Beach.** Taylor Library

RND in September 1914. Towards the end of March and the beginning of April 1915 squadrons of the Royal Naval Armoured Car Division were sent to the Eastern Mediterranean, comprising No. 3 Squadron, under the command of Josiah Wedgewood MP, from the family famous for their Staffordshire pottery, and No. 4 Squadron, under James Boothby. The cars were built on nothing but the best – the chassis was of Rolls Royce origin. With these two armoured car units were included No. 9, 10, 11 and 12 Motor Maxim Squadrons, which were motorcycle units with sidecars manned by men of the Royal Naval Air Service.

Leaving their Rolls Royce armoured cars behind, but taking twelve Motor cycles in order to transport their Maxims and help carry ammunition, 50 men from No. 3 Squadron RNACD under the command of Lieutenant-Commander Josiah Wedgewood with Sub-Lieutenants Hon. Arthur Coke MP, Illingworth and Parkes were detached to the SS River Clyde . Their task when the ship reached the beach was to provide covering fire to aid the landing of the troops.

By 20 April there were over 200 assorted vessels in Mudros Harbour - tramp steamers, tugs, hospital ships, ocean liners, warships and of course *SS River Clyde.* John Masefield wrote in *Gallipoli:*

In fine weather in Mudros a haze of beauty comes upon the hills and water till their loveliness is unearthly, it is so rare. Then the bay is like a blue jewel, and the hills lose their savagery, and glow, and are gentle, and the sun comes up from Troy, and the peaks of Samothrace change colour, and all the marvellous ships in the harbour are transfigured.

In fact the harbour at Mudros became so crowded that ships had to be sent to Tris Boukis Bay, Skyros. On 22 April various messages of encouragement were sent to the invading army. Brigadier General Hare, Covering Force Commander, issued a Special Order of the Day:

Ship's lantern dated 1914, found in Mudros Harbour.

Mudros Harbour, Lemnos, today.

Fusiliers! Our Brigade is to have the honour to be the first to land and to cover the disembarkation of the rest of the Division. Our task will be no easy one. Let us carry it through in a way worthy of the traditions of the distinguished regiments of which the Fusilier Brigade is composed; in such a way that the men of Albuhera and Minden, of Delhi and Lucknow, may hail us as their equals in valour and military achievement, and that future historians may say of us as Napier said of the Fusilier Brigade at Albuhera – 'Nothing could stop this astonishing Infantry.'

Security was famously lax in the build up to the landings, so very different from to-day's conflicts; rumour was rife and spies abounded everywhere. The landings were talked about openly in cities such as Cairo. A classic example of this can be found in Compton Mackenzie's *Gallipoli Memories*, when he waits impatiently in Capri for orders from Sir Ian Hamilton, having been gazetted (with the help of Edward Marsh, CB CMG CV, then serving in the Admiralty) as a lieutenant in the Royal Marines. He wrote:

What between trying to finish the book and grow a military moustache, suffering agonies from neuritis and imagining all the various obstacles that might prevent my helping to force the Dardanelles (our intention to do which was by now a topic of the Italian papers) I wonder I did not go permanently off my head.

By 24 April all preparations had been made. The men were raring to go. They were keen and enthusiastic, despite being told that the Turks would be a formidable foe and were not to be underestimated. From the evening of 23 April and on 24 April hundreds of ships were manoeuvring around the Mudros area and preparing to leave for their various destinations. General Hamilton was on board the HMS *Queen Elizabeth*, using it as his headquarters before moving off to Tenedos along with the men of the British Covering force. This included Major General Hunter-Weston, with his headquarters on HMS *Euryalys*, accompanied amongst others by HMS *Implacable* and HMS *Cornwallis*. The Anzacs were preparing to leave and go east of Imbros en route to Gaba Tepe, the Royal Naval Division to the Gulf of Saros for their diversionary attack, and the French going further south to the Asiatic shore for their own diversionary action. Orlo Williams, Chief Cipher Officer, aboard the *Arcadian*, captured the feeling at that time as he scribbled in his diary :

The SS River Clyde, *with her extra gangways tacked on her side and her sand-bagged upper structure, left Mudros for Tenedos, carrying her gallant company and Doughty-Wylie away, a great many of them forever. An atmosphere of intense excitement begins to be felt, and the emotion as the transports, crammed with troops, all cheering, moved down the roadstead in procession, as if proudly parading before action in front of the assembled shipping, was overwhelming. Tears rolled down my cheeks as those men went so gaily to their desperate enterprise.*

The ships moved quietly into the dark open sea and by 10.00 pm the Helles contingent had gathered west of Tekke Burnu, on the western coast of Cape Helles. In the very early hours of 25 April all the warships of the covering force were in their battle positions.

The men were roused and given a hot meal. They were then ordered to transfer to the small boats, which formed the tows which would take them to their destiny. The troops filed silently into the vulnerable craft, and sat upright, tense and silent. They had been practising for several weeks beforehand, carrying 200 SAA (small arms ammunition) and three days' iron rations in a pack which eventually weighed 88 pounds; but this was now the real thing.

At 5.00 am on Sunday 25th April the silence and intense stillness of the morning was broken by the Fleet, which opened up with a massive bombardment and the flotilla moved in. The vivid flashes from the guns, the smoke rolling in great clouds and the dull heavy sound of the firing meant that the battle had started.

A number of ships had been allocated as a covering force and they included:

Along the Straits - HMS *Vengeance* and HMS *Lord Nelson*
Along the Asiatic Coast - HMS *Prince George*
At Sedd El Bahr - HMS *Albion*
At Tekke Burnu - HMS *Swiftsure*

At V Beach HMS *Dublin*, HMS *Goliath*, HMS *Talbot* and HMS *Minerva*. The ships pounded the beach for an hour. Unfortunately, there was a delay between the ending of the Naval bombardment and

HMS *Albion*.

the landing of the boats, which gave valuable time for the Turkish infantry to recover, return to their positions in the trenches and man their machine guns, many of which overlooked the amphitheatre.

The plan called for X, W, V and S forces to land simultaneously. However, because of the differences in the tide, the trawlers towing S Force were delayed. Eventually X, W and V moved in before S. By now it was almost 6 am. With the sun shining brightly, the Fleet lifted its bombardment. There was a wonderful silence and absolutely no response from the shore.

The famous poems *Cargoes* and *Reynard the Fox* were probably learnt by heart by many at school, and the name of the poet and writer John Masefield well known. At the outbreak of the First World War John Masefield was 36 and a respected and well established writer. With patriotism burning in his heart he volunteered as a medical orderly for the British Red Cross and in August 1915 was on Gallipoli, working in a volunteer nautical ambulance service, with funds raised by himself.

A contemporary account, *Gallipoli,* was published in 1916 by John Masefield, as an answer to numerous questions and criticisms on the Dardanelles Campaign during a visit to the United States in 1916, where he had gone to win support for the Allies as well as to drum up medical aid:

> *Those who wish to imagine the scene must think of twenty miles of any rough and steep sea coast known to them, picturing it as roadless, waterless, much broken with gullies, covered with scrub, sandy, loose, and difficult to walk on, and without more than two miles of accessible landing throughout its length.*
>
> *Let them picture this familiar twenty miles dominated at intervals by three hills bigger than the hills about them, the north*

Officers 1/Royal Dublin Fusiliers, March 1915.

hill a peak, the centre a ridge or plateau, and the south hill a lump. Then let them imagine the hills entrenched, the landing mined, the beaches tangled with barbed wire, ranged by howitzers and swept by machine guns, and themselves three thousand miles from home, going out before dawn with rifles, packs, and water-bottles, to pass the mines under shell fire, cut through the wire under machine-gun fire, clamber up the hills under the fire of all arms, by the glare of shell-bursts, in the withering and crashing tumult of modern war, and then to dig themselves in a waterless and burning hill while more numerous enemy charge them with the bayonet.

And let them imagine themselves enduring this night after night, day after day, without rest or solace, nor respite from the peril of death, seeing their friends killed, and the position imperilled, getting their food, their munitions, even their drink, from the jaws of death, and their breath from the taint of death, and their brief sleep upon the dust of death. Let them imagine themselves driven mad by heat and toil and thirst by day, shaken by frost at midnight, weakened by disease and broken by pestilence, yet rising on the word with a shout and going forward to die in exultation in a cause foredoomed and almost hopeless.

Only then will they begin, even dimly, to understand what our seizing and holding of the landings meant.

It was not until after 6.00am that the first part of the Covering Force came ashore. Included were two and a half companies 1/RDF and No 4 Platoon Anson Battalion due for V Beach, and two platoons of the Royal Dublin Fusiliers, who were to storm the Camber, a small landing place sheltered by a cliff overhang east of Sedd El Bahr. These troops had disembarked from the Cross Channel cargo boat, designated Fleet

Sweeper No1, as soon as she had reached her position off V Beach at daybreak and boarded their four tows alongside, each consisting of one steamboat and four cutters all ready for the landing.

Nearby were 1/Royal Munster Fusiliers, two companies 2/ Hampshires, one company of Royal Dublin Fusiliers, No 13 Platoon Anson Battalion and various other sub units, all aboard the *SS River Clyde* due to arrive a few minutes after the first wave. However, a strong current held up the small tows which in effect meant that both parties arrived simultaneously. The massive *SS River Clyde*, recently painted partly yellow and the flotilla of small boats moved gently to the shore at the same time. All was quiet, with nothing seen or heard from the shore

As noted by the *Official History*, the following words were scribbled in the diary of Lieutenant Colonel W. de L. Williams, senior Staff Officer on *SS River Clyde*, as the ship approached the shore.

06.10 am Within half a mile of the shore. We are far ahead of the tows. No OC Troops on board. It must cause a mix up, if we, the 2nd line, arrive before the 1st line. With difficulty I get Unwin to swerve off and await the tows.

6.22 am Ran smoothly ashore without a tremor. No opposition. We shall land unopposed.

How wrong he was. With an awful crash, the terrible fusillade began. A tornado of fire swept the beach as the men began disembarking from

Landing on V Beach.

the vulnerable wooden boats. Heavy casualties took place in the first few minutes, there being no escaping the deadly and accurate Turkish fire. There had been no element of surprise. The men desperately stumbled, floundering uncontrollably with their sodden kit in the shallow water, crying out with pain as they were hit continuously with bullets that splashed viciously across the water. The sea turned crimson. There were piles of corpses lying at grotesque angles at the gently lapping water's edge and prostrated in gruesome groups in front of the barbed wire – grim witness to the fact that in spite of the decimating fire, a few Royal Dublin Fusiliers actually make it onto the sand.

The little boats, now full of dead and dying, drifted away from the beach. Within a matter of minutes the 700 strong first wave of 1/RDF had lost almost 50% casualties, and most of the remaining men were so badly wounded they would play no further part in the action that day.

One of the early casualties who made it to the shore, but was killed almost instantly, was the Commanding Officer of the 1/RDF, Lieutenant Colonel Rooth. An eye witness, Captain Molony of W Company, wrote later:

..the slaughter was terrific. Most of the officers were killed or wounded. Colonel Rooth, the CO, was shot dead at the edge of the water; Major Featherstonhaugh, second in command, was mortally wounded in his boat; Captain Johnson badly wounded while still in his boat; Captain French, the biggest man in the Battalion, got ashore with a bullet in the arm; Captain Anderson was shot dead on the beach, and many others were wounded...It was a terrible affair, and a few minutes of such fire decimated the Battalion. The people who got ashore

Lt Col R A Rooth CO 1/Royal Dublin Fusiliers.

established themselves on the beach as best they could under a bank which ran along the shore for some distance and was from four to five feet high.[1]

The Regiment were told of the death of many of their officers, including their Commanding Officer and Adjutant, at about 10.00 am that morning. As Colonel Wylly quotes in *Neill's Blue Caps:*

The effect of the news of Colonel Rooth's death could be read plainly on the faces of all ranks, as they had such faith in him as their commanding officer, and would have followed him to the ends of the earth.

An eye witness, Lieutenant Maffett of X Company, whose experiences epitomised the horrors of that day, spoke of how all the sailors in his boat were killed or wounded. His men grabbed the oars and the boat drifted broadside towards the beach. As it grounded, the boat, already half full of water from bullet holes, was hit with incendiary shells and began to catch fire.   He continued:

> Several of the men who had been wounded fell to the bottom of the boat, and were either drowned there or suffocated by other men falling on top of them; many, to add to their death agonies, were burnt as well. We then grounded, and I jumped out of the bows of the boat and got hit on the head, other bullets going into a pack that I was carrying on my shoulders. I went under water and came up again, and tried to encourage the men to get to the shore and under cover as fast as they could as it was their only chance. I then went under again. Someone caught hold of me and began pulling me ashore.Looking back out to sea I saw the remnants of my platoon trying to get to the shore, but they were shot down one after another, and their bodies drifted out to sea or lay immersed a few feet from the shore. [2]

Men drowned as they were shot in three feet of water. Some eventually managed to reach the safety of the low sand bank, about four to five feet high, a few yards from the edge of the water, and took shelter there.   Very few of the wooden rowing boats were left undamaged.

Lt J B Dodge, an American serving with the Hood Battalion RND.

Lieutenant CW Maffett was fortunate, he was to survive the Campaign and the Great War and on the disbandment of the RDF in 1922 transferred to the Black Watch.

The Royal Naval Division were also in the forefront of this horror. In his capacity as an assistant Naval Landing Officer at V Beach, Sub Lieutenant Johnny Dodge, an American serving with Hood Battalion, accompanied 1/RDF as they landed in that maelstrom of fire. He was wounded before he even reached the shore, but remained on the beach

The low sandy bank on V Beach below which the troops sheltered on 25.4.15.

throughout that day, indeed until the afternoon of 26 April, stalwartly carrying out his task. He was eventually awarded the DSC for his efforts during that trying time. He transferred to the Army in April 1916, achieved the rank of Lieutenant Colonel and, surviving the War, went into politics, but failed in his bid to become an MP.

Lieutenant Colonel Tizard, commanding 1/RMF, helplessly had to

Photogragh taken from the S*S River Clyde* shows the dead and wounded on board from earlier fighting and a party of 1/Royal Dublin Fusiliers taking cover behind a low bank on V Beach.

watch the carnage from the *SS River Clyde* as 1/RDF tried to get ashore. He knew that he would have to send his men into the same hell.

The death, too, of the first priest to be killed in action, a much loved and respected Roman Catholic Chaplain, also caused grief and great sadness particularly amongst the men of the Royal Dublin Fusiliers.

Father William Joseph Finn, born in Yorkshire in 1875 into a family originally from County Tipperary, Ireland, was ordained in 1900 and became a Chaplain 4th Class with the Battalion in late 1914. On the day before the landings he had held services on the transport ships, and given Holy Communion. The next day he requested permission from Lieutenant Colonel Rooth to land on the beach with the men. The Colonel was very reluctant to allow this, and tried to dissuade him. However there was eventually no answer to his persistence and his assertion that he knew his place was beside the dying soldier and that he had to go. He felt he had become one of them and wanted to share their difficulties and dangers.

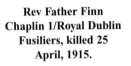

As the boats drew nearer to the beach the awful hail of machine gun and rifle fire, together with shrapnel, took its toll. Father Finn, in the same boat as the Commanding Officer, leapt over the side to go to the assistance of wounded and dying men. His clothes were ripped with bullets and he was hit. Despite the pain he endured, he

Rev Father Finn Chaplin 1/Royal Dublin Fusiliers, killed 25 April, 1915.

Telegram reporting death of Rev W. Finn.

A ○ *l℔u w*	**POST OFFICE**		**TELEGRAPHS.**	3ʊ 4 ·/5
	(Inland Official)		Telegrams only.)	No. of Telegram
ʼrefix____Code____				I certify that this Telegram is sent on the service of the
Office of Origin and Service Instructions.		Words.	Sent	**WAR OFFICE.**
O. H. M. S.			At_____.M.	
			To_____	
			By____	(Signature)

Attention is called to the Regulations printed at the back hereof.   Dated Stamp.

| **TO** { *1. Finn B₂ 448 Holderness road Hull* |
| *deeply* | Regret | to | inform | you | that |
| | *R C Chaplain Revᵈ W. Finn ⟶ reported* |
| *Alexandria Khan Bean killed actn 25ᵗʰ April. Lord* |
| *Kitchener expresses his sympathy* |

FROM { Secretary, War Office.

The Name and Address of the Sender, IF NOT TO BE TELEGRAPHED, should be written in the space provided at the Back of the Form.

was seen crawling about the beach talking quietly to the RDF and trying to give Absolution to those close to death. This was not without the greatest difficulty, as one account states, as he had to hold his wounded right arm up with his left. He suffered from loss of blood and eventually exhaustion, and eye witness accounts attest that within a short time he was killed by shrapnel.

In his book *With the Twenty-Ninth Division in Gallipoli* his friend, the Reverend Creighton, a Church of England padre, wrote:

> *The men never forgot him and were never tired of speaking about him. ..I am told they kept his helmet for a very long time after and carried it with them wherever they went.*

The following few lines from a poem written by Bertrand Shadwell of Chicago sum up the feelings at the time:

> *O the boys are all in tears*
> *In the Dublin Fusiliers -*
> *They have lost the friend of years,*
> *Father Finn*

As recorded in an article in Volume 7 of the *Journal of the Royal Dublin Fusiliers Association,* Father Finn was buried by Father Harker of the Royal Munster Fusiliers. The grave was marked with a cross made out of an ammunition box with a simple inscription. Today he lies in V Beach Cemetery, next to Lieutenant Colonel Rooth.

There was chaos on *SS River Clyde*. Because of the evasive action taken by Commander Unwin, the collier had beached further out than it had been hoped. To add to his dismay, Unwin saw the steam hopper, which was to form the main link between ship and shore lying uselessly grounded on his port side, broadside on the beach and some 15 yards from the bow of the big ship. Aware of the danger of this failure and any delay, he immediately decided to make a bridge of the lighters so that the men could get ashore.

So began the momentous actions of great courage which were to culminate in the award of Victoria Crosses for actions on V Beach to Commander Edward Unwin, Midshipman George Drewry, Midshipman Wilfred Malleson, Able Seaman William Charles Williams (the first posthumous Royal Navy VC a Boer War veteran, being present at the Relief of Ladysmith and the Battle of the Tugela Heights), Seaman George Samson and Sub Lieutenant Arthur Tisdall (RND).

20 year old Midshipman George Drewry watched in helpless frustration as he saw the first wave

Midshipman George L. Drewry RNR.

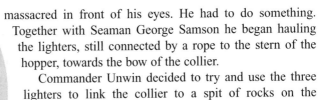

massacred in front of his eyes. He had to do something. Together with Seaman George Samson he began hauling the lighters, still connected by a rope to the stern of the hopper, towards the bow of the collier.

Commander Unwin decided to try and use the three lighters to link the collier to a spit of rocks on the starboard side of the ship, which gave direct access to the shore. With Able Seaman William C. Williams, he stepped onto the lighters and tried to get them as close to the rocks as he could. When it was obvious that the pinnace he was using could go no further without grounding, Commander Unwin jumped into the sea, pulling the lighters with a line, standing waist deep in water, exposed to heavy fire but desperately trying to keep the bridge intact.

Able Seaman W C Williams RN.

During these desperate moments, fully exposed to a continuous hail of fire, Midshipman Drewry, who had managed to get ashore, waded back into the water when he realised what Commander Unwin was trying to do and went to his assistance, bringing more rope.

Williams had stuck close to the Commander and together they had put a gangplank across two of the lighters and by dint of swimming and wading managed to get ashore, pulling the lighters behind them. The first lighter was at last within a few yards of the beach. Despite the appalling Turkish fire, to their eternal credit, there they stayed, waist-deep in water, holding the precarious 'bridge' in place. Commander Unwin then yelled back to the *SS River Clyde* for the landing to begin.

In the Westminster Gazette, Josiah Wedgewood MP wrote

It was the Munsters (sic) that charged first with a sprig of shamrock in their caps, then the Dublins, Worcesters, Hampshires – it was the maxims and pom poms at Sedd El Bahr that kept our heads down. Dead Munsters lying in neat rows. clothing set alight by rifle fire, causing agony to the wounded.

It was now the turn of the 1/Royal Munster Fusiliers. Two assaulting companies, X Company under Captain Geddes and Z Company under Captain Henderson, were ordered ashore Together with some of the 2/Hants, they poured eagerly down the gangplanks onto the lighters – to certain death. Z Company under Captain Henderson exited down the starboard side and were met by a withering fire which hammered into them and they were decimated, suffering many casualties, shot or

Lt. Col. G Geddes, DSO 1/Royal Munster Fusiliers.

drowned. Captain Henderson was shot twice on the beach and died of wounds in Egypt almost three weeks later. Captain Geddes led his Company out on the port side. The first 48 men behind him all fell, machined gunned by the enemy, but he managed to swim to the shore, knowing that many of his men behind him were dragged down by their heavy packs and drowned. Exhausted after his efforts and hardly able to move, he eventually managed to crawl towards cover about ten yards from the beach and join some of the 1/RDF, sodden, cold and hardly able to believe the horror of what was happening. At about 7.00 am he began to move his surviving men to the right flank in the general direction of the Old Fort (also known as Fort No3) at Sedd El Bahr, although this meant charging through a gap in the sandbank. Captain Geddes himself was shot through the shoulder at this time but was able to dig in, where he was joined by the 14 survivors of the 1/RDF Camber party together with three survivors of Z Company RMF. Any further progress at this time proved impossible.

Shortly after the survivors had managed to reach the beach, the bridge was broken. Able Seaman Williams, who had been courageously and desperately holding on to the rope next to Commander Unwin for over an hour, was shot as he stood breast deep in the water and let the rope go. Commander Unwin carried him back to the lighter, but it was too late – Williams died in his arms.

Surgeon P. Burrowes Kelly DSO RN wrote warmly of this young man:

> He was the pride of our ship's company, and described by
> Commander Unwin as the bravest sailor he had ever met.

In the absence of the bridge, which had now drifted away from the beach, men jumped into the sea and were dragged down by their packs and equipment. All attempts to land and make progress failed, despite determined efforts to maintain the floating bridge. Midshipman Drewry had some success in pulling a rope from one of the lighters to the outlying rocks. Commander Unwin, now very cold, collapsed from his strenuous efforts, which is hardly surprising in a man of 51, and Midshipman Drewry dragged him onto the lighter from where he was taken aboard the collier. The shelling continued and George Drewry saw with his own eyes the dead and wounded on the lighter and around the spit of rocks, where the sea around it for some yards was red. If the men were not killed trying to reach the shore, they were killed on the exposed beach, before being able to dig in.

Together with Lieutenant Morse, in command of a 38 strong group from *HMS Cornwallis*, whose task it was to ferry the reinforcements of the third tow of boats to the shore, Drewry went aboard the third lighter.

The most immediate task now was to restore the bridge, which was essential to the landing operation. Midshipman Wilfrid Malleson, at 18 years old, destined to become the youngest VC of the Gallipoli Campaign, was in one of the boats making up the third tow and approached V Beach about 7.00 am. The men had then to transfer to the lighters under continuous fire from the shore. He saw Drewry's lighter being pushed into position, but saw that it was not secured at the rear to the steam hopper. He then saw Drewry fall, hit by shrapnel in the head, and as blood poured down his face, going in to the engine room of the hopper and have his wound bandaged. He then returned and determinedly jumped overboard with a line between his teeth and began to swim towards the lighter.

Midshipman Malleson, intently watching, soon realised that the exhausted Drewry was in difficulties as the current was very strong and the rope he had snatched too short. Malleson found some more rope – but only by dint of retrieving it, in full view of the enemy and under fire, from its original position where it had kept the three lighters against the spit of rocks, and then swam with the rope himself. The line broke and he had to make two further attempts, neither of which proved successful but a Lieutenant Morse eventually made the lighters fast and at last a new bridge had been formed.

Midshipman W St Aubyn Malleson RN, attempting to secure a drifting barge at V Beach.

There is a succinct two line entry in the *War Diary of the 29th Division* for the actions early that morning:

Gallipoli Peninsula 25th April 7.am River Clyde, under light shell fire grounded some way out from Beach V, and lighters forming pier to the shore were pushed out. The tows with Dublin Fusiliers pulled in at the same time.

Lieutenant Commander Samson RNAS flew over the beaches that morning. He noticed that the colour of the sea appeared unusual and flew lower to take a closer look. For fifty yards out it was red with blood.

By now it was 9.00 am. and Drewry,

Malleson and Commander Unwin were all in the sick bay on the *SS River Clyde*, shivering uncontrollably from a combination of the cold, exposure and the horrors of the day.

Commander Unwin then defied the doctors, got up, found a boat and continued to make several journeys, picking up wounded men from the shallow water. Even he had to give up eventually, suffering from complete exhaustion, and it was a miracle that, although he was hit at least three times, he managed to survive the heaviest fire poured down from the shore.

Midshipman Drewry, having already had a colourful young life, survived all the rigours of the Gallipoli campaign, including involvement in the Suvla landings, only to die from the result of a fatal accident when commanding his own ship HM *William Jackson* in August 1918. A block fell from a derrick and hit him heavily on the head, fracturing his skull and breaking his left arm.

There were many heroes that day, not least Seaman George McKenzie Samson, who initially had assisted the officers in trying to make a bridge to the shore. He then spent most of that day helping the wounded and getting them to shelter from the exposed beach and had many narrow escapes from death. Little chance was given for his survival. But survive he did, and he was awarded the Victoria Cross for his brave actions.

Seaman G McKenzie Samson RNR.

Surgeon P Burrowes-Kelly, DSO, RN wrote:

(Seaman Samson) was most prominent throughout 25 and 26 April. He effected many daring rescues of the wounded, stowed them carefully away in the hopper, and treated them himself until medical assistance was forthcoming. In the intervals he devoted his time to attending to snipers. He was eventually covered by a Maxim and wounded in nineteen distinct places. Had the unique experience of being presented with a white feather (many months afterwards) about three hours

SS River Clyde with the floating bridge formed by small boats.

Sub Lt A W St Clair Tisdall RNVR.

before his public reception on his return to his native town of Carnoustie.

He was discharged from the Navy in June 1916 for a year because of his terrible wounds: he never rejoined, but after the war he served with the Merchant Navy until 1923, when he contracted pneumonia and died.

Another hero that day was Sub Lieutenant Arther Waldern St. Clair Tisdall RNVR, Anson Battalion RND, who on 27 April that year sent a postcard to his family saying:

Have been under fire and are now ashore; all day spent in burying soldiers. Some of my men are killed. We are all happy and fit. Plenty of hard work and enemy shells, and a smell of dead men.

Born in Bombay in 1890 into a well established and respected Irish family, Tisdall spent his early childhood in Persia (now Iran) where his father worked at the Church Missionary Society's Persian Baghdad Mission. Little did he realise when he sailed through the Dardanelles when he was ten on his way to school in England that he would be fighting there fifteen years later with the Royal Naval Division. He had a retiring personality, and was known as a gentle, modest, quietly spoken person, highly regarded amongst his friends.

For such an 'ordinary' person he performed acts of extraordinary courage on 25th April, when during the landing from the *SS River Clyde* he heard wounded men on the beach and on the rocks crying out for help. He could stand their distress no longer, and jumped into the water to try and rescue some of them, pushing a boat in front of him. With assistance from five colleagues, he waded into water up to his neck and made between four and five trips under very accurate and heavy fire. His innate sense of duty enabled him to save the lives of several wounded men. In all the maelstrom and confusion of that day it was not until a year later that the identity of this gallant young man was confirmed, and he was awarded a posthumous Victoria Cross. It is poignant to record that he never knew of this award, as he was killed at Krithia on May 6 1915, aged 24. His name is recorded on the Helles Memorial. His Victoria Cross is in the safe hands of the London Division, RNVR.

As a result of these acts of continuous courage and gallantry, lives which undoubtedly would have been lost were saved, and a grim situation made a little less grim.

Regarding the half company 1/RDF who were in the first part of the Covering Force, they had landed safely at the Camber but were met by

The Camber today.

fierce opposition and many of the raiding party were killed, including all their officers. The few men who succeeded in reaching Sedd El Bahr were overpowered, and the attack failed. A party of about 14 dug in near the village whilst a small number managed to return to the Camber. With no officers surviving, they realised they had no choice but to signal to HMS *Queen Elizabeth* to be re-embarked. A picket boat was eventually sent and they were rescued. The dead bodies of their comrades were found in the village the next day.

At about 8.00 am Major Jarrett 1/RMF took his Y Company ashore, but also suffered severe casualties. From the Turks' excellent defensive position, it would not have been difficult to get the range of the huge ship and they had commanding views of the British attempts to reach the beach. Once ashore, Major Jarrett immediately realised the serious difficulties that prevailed and that any further attempts to land would be suicidal. Accordingly he sent a message with one of his officers, Lieutenant Nightingale, back to *SS River Clyde*, suggesting that no further attempts should be made to land, certainly until darkness fell. Lieutenant Colonel Carington Smith 2/Hampshires, senior officer on *SS River Clyde*, agreed.

Some valued protection had been given by the machine guns of No. 3 Squadron, Royal Naval Armoured Car Division, under Commander Josiah Wedgewood, which were set up in the bows. He was to write shortly afterwards to Winston Churchill:

> *The wounded cried out all day - in every boat, lighter, hopper and all along the shore. It was horrible, and all within 200 yards of our guns.*

Now came confusion. Upon receiving misleading information regarding the so called success of the landings to date, the GOC 29th Division ordered the landing of the main body at 8.30 am and for 1/Essex to be disembarked at W Beach instead of V.

141

Therefore, whilst 1/Border began to land at X Beach and 1/Essex at W Beach, a fleet sweeper carrying part of the main force namely Brigadier General Napier and 88 Brigade Staff, two Platoons 4/Worcesters and two companies 2/Hampshires, not realising the true position at V, crept in and waited offshore for some small boats to take them to the beach. Because so many of these boats had been badly damaged, they had to wait some time.

The little boats, these unsung heroes, ran the gauntlet of devastating fire time and time again in an effort to assist the wounded and dying soldiers on the beach. The crews, despite facing instant death, staunchly continued this work without respite. Eventually one came along with only space for General Napier, the commander of the main force, his staff and a few soldiers. As they approached the shore an officer on the *SS River Clyde* shouted frantically that it was impossible to land. General Napier yelled back: 'I'll have a damned good try'.

Undeterred, Brigadier General Napier jumped into a lighter, a larger boat filled with men that was closest to him, and shouted at them to pull hard for shore. No effort was made to carry out his command, and it was then that he realised with a sickening heart that all the men were dead.

The General and his staff managed to reach the steam hopper close to the beach, but after fifteen minutes, under terrible fire, both Brigadier General Napier and his Brigade Major Captain Costeker, were killed. It was a waste of two of the most valuable and experienced men present that day. Lieutenant Colonel Carington Smith, 2/Hants, was also killed during the afternoon as he was looking through his binoculars on the bridge of the *SS River Clyde*.

Then for long hours the remainder stayed on board, down below in the grounded steamer, while the shots beat on her plates with a rattling clang which never stopped.

The *SS River Clyde* was fired upon continuously, but fortunately little damaged had been done. Work had already been carried out to protect the armoured car detachment and their guns, with steel casements being constructed, the bridge lined with steel plates and other parts protected with sandbags. With the possible threat now of the enemy storming the ship, the men of the RNAS assisted in the urgent building of barricades on deck. Their 12 machine guns fired almost continuously throughout that day. It could perhaps be said that the landing here was saved from complete disaster by these machine guns. But now ammunition levels were beginning to run frighteningly low. Very little could really be done to assist those now taking cover by the sandbank on the beach. Certain death would follow any who tried to leave the ship. At this time there were still about 1000 men on board the *SS River Clyde.*

General Sir Ian Hamilton advised the GOC 29th Division of the situation and it was then, at about mid-morning, that he ordered 4/Worcesters and two companies 2/Hants to W Beach.

Despite the earlier advice of Lieutenant Colonel Carington Smith, who advised waiting until dark before making any more attempts to land more troops that day, one more attempt was made to get Lieutenant Nightingale 1/RMF, and his remaining platoons ashore, the objective being to gain the high ground on the western side of the cove.

But it was an impossible task. At the first sign of movement, devastating fire broke out. It was all the men could do to reach the sandy bank and a degree of safety.

Lt Col H Carrington-Smith, 2/Hampshire Regiment
Royal Hampshire Regimental Journal

It was not going to be possible to advance from V Beach until the high ground between there and W Beach had been captured.

A tremendous bombardment from the three battleships recommenced at 5.30 pm. Dust, smoke and flames poured out of the village, the high ground behind the beach shook as earth rose upwards and part of the Old Fort was hit again.

The diary of HMS *Queen Elizabeth* states:

All day we bombarded the forts and entrenchments surrounding the beach with 15-inch and 6-inch, as did the other supporting ships, but never saw any sign of an enemy, who maintained a heavy fire on our men ashore, those working the water at the lighters and on the River Clyde.

We also bombarded the ruined village of Sedd El Bahr and very soon set it on fire, but failed to eject some of the numerous snipers who were installed there.

Major C Jarrett 1/RMF, then led about 120 of his men, together with a few 2/Hants along the beach and tried to occupy the Old Fort. But the Turks were still there, grimly manning their machine gun. There was no way through, and the troops had to withdraw outside the walls and take cover. He set up a simple line of outposts and at dusk was carefully checking that these were in place when he was shot in the throat, and died almost instantly. He was buried on the beach early on the morning of 26 April and today lies in Lancashire Landing Cemetery. (His brother, Captain Jarret DSO, died of wounds received just over three weeks later in Belgium and is buried in Hop Store Cemetery, Vlamertinghe.)

As the night began to close in, the village of Sedd El Bahr burned brightly. A few troops hung on precariously whilst bodies lay everywhere in distorted agony.

After dark, work started in disembarking the remaining men from the *SS River Clyde*, who then joined the survivors on the beach. The appalling task of clearing the dead and wounded from the beach and gangways then commenced. As Lieutenant Colonel Rooth 1/RDF had been killed whilst disembarking earlier in the day, command was now given to Lieutenant Colonel Tizard 1/RMF.

Major Beckwith, now the senior surviving officer of 2/Hants, ordered a reconnaissance ashore. The main difficulty on the right flank was that Hill 141 remained in Turkish hands, and whilst this was so there could be no advance on Achi Baba.

At dusk on 25 April X Beach and W Beach had been linked up with the capture of Hills 114 and 138 – the extent of the ground gained by the British at Helles that day. A high price was paid for that achievement.

From time to time the authors have had the opportunity of approaching V Beach by sea, and together with friends, have held a simple commemorative service on the water. It is an emotive experience to hear the echoes of the Last Post played by a regimental bugler in memory of all those who landed on that infamous day and to see the poppy leaves that are thrown from the boat stain the water red.

Sedd El Bahr in ruins, early May 1915.

The *Official History* sums up by vividly describing what could be called a scene from Hades:

So the long day ended. Night closed in on that unforgettable scene with the thin line of tired troops still clinging to their precarious position, the sombre silhouette of ridge and fort still barring their advance, and the burning village reddening sea and sky. And it was here that two months earlier a handful of marines had landed without a casualty.

26 APRIL 1915

Dawn broke on 26 April with the survivors of the carnage the previous day

144

still crouched under the shelter of the sandbank. Badly shaken, the troops had spent a cold, miserable night, and it had rained. Many of them had been involved in fighting during the night, they had had little or no sleep and almost nothing to eat.

Sir Ian Hamilton recalled:

> *The remnant of the landing party still crouched on the beach beneath the shelter of the sandy escarpment which had saved so many lives. With them were two officers of my General Staff - Lieutenant Colonel Doughty-Wylie and Lieutenant Colonel Williams. These two officers, who had landed from the* River Clyde, *had been striving, with conspicuous contempt for danger, to keep all their comrades in good heart during this day and night of ceaseless imminent peril.*

Although the Turks appeared to have pulled back beyond Fort No 1, they still held the village of Sedd El Bahr and Hill 141, with about three companies, with their snipers and a machine gun in the Old Fort.

Major Beckwith, with some of his 2/Hampshires fresh from the SS *River Clyde,* was then ordered to attack on the right with the aim being the capture of these three main objectives; whilst on the left a mixed force of Dublins and Munsters were ordered to link up with the men from W Beach, who had penetrated the barbed wire.

Finally, an attack would be made in the centre through the barbed wire obstacles towards Hill 141.

The Royal Navy bombardment was aimed to the far side of the village and a considerable amount of damage was done until the fort and village were in ruins. Fighting from cover to cover and dodging Turkish shells and snipers, the landing party made their way inland and, at last, the Old Fort was taken, but there the advance was halted.

As it seemed that the attack had lost its impetus, three staff oficers decided to go ashore and assist. They were the two staff officers from the SS *River Clyde,* Lieutenant Colonel Weir de Lancy Williams, Liason Officer Operations and Lieutenant Colonel Doughty-Wylie, Liaison Officer Intelligence, as well as Captain Walford, Brigade Major 29th Division Artillery, but seconded as a Staff Officer to Colonel Tizard. Lieutenant Colonel Doughty-Wylie and Captain Walford (assisted by Captain Addison, 2/Hampshires) set out from the gateway of the Old Fort whilst Lieutenant Colonel Williams went to the left hand side of the beach.

It was a grim day. Met by incessant and accurate fire from the determined Turkish defenders, Captain Walford, at the head of a group of men, led them up into the village. The spasmodic advance involved desperate house to house fighting and Captain Walford threw himself into these efforts to clear Sedd El Bahr.

> *They had to encounter a most stubborn resistance, and suffered heavy losses from the fire of cleverly-concealed riflemen and machine guns.*

> *But though many fell, their comrades, supported by the terrific fire from the huge naval guns, continued to press on, breaking in the doors of the houses with the butts of their rifles and routing the snipers out of their hiding-places at the point of the bayonet.* [3]

A foothold was gained in the village by about 10.00 am and by midday the troops had reached the northern outskirts, and the men were in position ready to attack the Old Castle/barracks on Hill 141. Sadly, by this time, both Captain Walford and Captain Addison had been killed.

Garth Neville Walford had already had two close encounters with death during the Retreat from Mons in August 1914, whilst serving with the Royal Field Artillery. October 1914 found him in the vicinity of Ypres and in January 1915 he took up his new appointment with the new 29th Division as Brigade Major Royal Artillery. As did many of his friends who sailed for the Dardanelles that April, he remembered his classical education and in his last letter home five days before he was killed, a feeling of a great idealistic romantic adventure comes through,

> *just like the Greek fleet going to Troy, people collected from all over the known world; we have even got our wooden horse, which I will explain later on.*

Captain Walford was initially buried near where he was killed, by the walls of the Old Fort in the village; and a large cross was placed on his grave, which remained there throughout the Campaign. When the

Original grave of Captain G Walford amid ruins of Sedd El Bahr.

CWGC cemetery was made on V Beach, his remains were re-interred there.

Back on V Beach itself, there now appears another hero on this scene – this time a 6' 6" Irish giant by the name of Corporal William Cosgrove. He had landed with 1/RMF and had seen the companies who had charged with him from the *SS River Clyde* suffer heavily. Those who managed to survive had to shelter under that infamous bank for the remainder of that day and the night that followed, tense, worn out and hungry.

The main problem was that the Turks still had machine guns and rifles determinedly covering the middle of V Beach. It was going to be almost a monumental task to try and make a path through the impregnable wall of barbed wire about forty yards from the beach. The wire was held up by tall, strong posts. But a breach had to be made in the wire to allow troops to go forward and assist in the attacks leading up towards Hill 141. A gap in the wire was made by a party from 1/RMF, the action described by Corporal Cosgrove:

**Cpl W Cosgrove
1/Royal Munster
Fusiliers.**

Our Sergeant Major was killed – a bullet through the brain. I then took charge; shouted to the boys to come on...The dash was quite 100 yards, and I don't know whether I ran or prayed the faster -...The wire was of great strength, strained as tight as a fiddle-string, and so full of spikes or thorns that you could not get the cutters between.

'"Heavens,' said I, 'we're done'; a moment later I threw the pliers from me, 'Pull them up,' I roared, 'put your arms round them and pull them out of the ground'..I believe there was wild cheering when they saw what I was at, but I only heard the screech of bullets...I could not tell how many I pulled up. I did

Barbed wire at Sedd El Bahr.

my best, and the boys that were left with me were every bit as good as myself.

Surgeon Burrowes-Kelly RN DSO describes these events graphically:

An Irish Giant. With his officers and brother Tommies dying and dead around him, he continued a task he had set himself of clearing a way through the Turkish wire. Though under heavy fire he continued at his task, and eventually, aided by his exceptional strength, succeeded in wrenching a stanchion out of the ground. The others had failed to cut the wire. The manner in which the man worked out in the open will never be forgotten by those who were fortunate enough to witness it.

What a sight that must have been – that huge mountain of a man tearing up the strong posts with his bare hands. At last a breach was made, and the Turkish trenches reached. This charge had resulted in a 200 yard length of trench being taken and 700 yards gained from the beach. Corporal Cosgrove was seriously wounded in the back in this attempt and was taken to a hospital in Malta. Many saw this wonderful act of sheer courage in face of almost certain death, and Corporal Cosgrove was awarded the Victoria Cross, warmly endorsed by Major General Hunter-Weston.

However, as the morning had worn on, it was apparent that the attack on Hill 141 from the left hand side had made no progress. Lieutenant Colonel Doughty-Wylie, who had been assisting Major Beckwith 2/Hampshires on the right hand side, came over with fifty reinforcements and at about midday took command of the varied assortment of troops, mainly RMF and RDF. The advance began, with desperate fighting with bayonets to take the houses to the left of the Old Fort.

Once the village of Sedd El Bahr had been completely taken, Lieutenant Colonel Doughty-Wylie asked for a naval bombardment on the Turkish positions that remained before he ordered the assault on Hill 141. He watched the shells fall from his position in the Old Fort. His main concern and determination now was that the strong redoubt, formerly a castle and since a renovated barracks, now disused, on top of the hill should be taken and, with a confidence that soon instilled itself into the tired troops with him, outlined his plan. He wanted the Hill to be attacked simultaneously after the end of the bombardment.

Now keen, enthusiastic and galvanised into action, the men hardly waited for the order to fix bayonets and, courageously led by Lt Colonel Doughty-Wylie and Major CTW Grimshaw commanding Z Company 1/RDF, they charged together in a great mass, cheering

Lt Colonel CHM Doughty-Wylie RWF leading the charge through Sedd El Bahr towards Hill 141 and its old castle, for which actions he was posthumously awarded the VC.

Major CTW Grimshaw DSO 1/Royal Dublin Fusiliers.

Lt Col CHM Doughty-Wylie.
Royal Welch Fusiliers Regimental Museum

wildly and racing for the summit of the Hill. They passed through barbed wire entanglements and deserted Turkish trenches to the crest, a flat area surrounded by a moat twenty feet deep which had just one way through. The Turks could be seen fleeing down through their communication trenches towards Achi Baba. It was now just after 2.00 pm. In an assault which took little over half an hour, at last it could be said that V Beach had been made secure. A difficult and dangerous situation had been averted. Hunter Weston's message sent at 2.35 pm rings with a huge sense of relief:

> *Our men swarming into old castle. Push forward to your right*
> *to join hands and consolidate your position.*

But success had its price.

Hill 141 and the old castle/barracks where Lt Col Doughty-Wylie fell.

On Hill 141, looking across Morto Bay to De Tott's battery.

With the position almost won, Lieutenant. Colonel Doughty-Wylie who, with a little cane in his hand, had led the attack all the way up from the beach through the west side of the village, under a galling fire, was shot through the brain while leading the last assault

According to eye witnesses, despite having a narrow escape when on his way from the Old Fort to the village, he was seen carrying no weapon of any kind, no rifle or bayonet, but just a small cane.

The success on V Beach on 26 April was due to a great extent to his leadership and that of Captain Walford, and this was warmly endorsed by Hunter Weston when he vowed to recommend them for a posthumous award, and in his view,

They achieved the impossible. They showed themselves Englishmen in the old mould.

Major Grimshaw was also killed on the summit of Hill 141. He had served in the British Army since 1897, including service in the Boer War, where he had been mentioned in despatches twice. He was also awarded the DSO. Together with many of his comrades, he is commemorated in V Beach Cemetery.

V Beach was at last secured by about 3.00 pm, the remainder of 26 April was spent in consolidation, and by the evening the situation was a great deal better than the evening before, but still tenuous. At last a footing had been gained, the Allies now held ground running from the coast at X Beach up to Sedd El Bahr and De Tott's Battery.

More importantly, about 18,500 troops of the 29th Division and other units were now ashore, together with a number of French battalions. Guns had been landed, not without difficulty, and were often manhandled from the beach inland by already exhausted troops, as the horses were unfit after such a long stay on board ship. Essential stores and supplies, including ammunition and water, were beginning to arrive on W and X Beaches. Tanks, fed by water lighters, especially ensured an improvement in the water supply on land. W Beach in particular began to look like a huge supply depot.

Dead turks among the ruins of the village of Sedd El Bahr, April 1915. Taylor Library

But the original hope that the whole of the 29th Division would be landed in 60 hours was dashed. Because of the great difficulties experienced; the shelling, the soft sand at the water's edge, the lack of steamboats, the cramped area available and the limited access from the beach itself and, above all, the chronic shortage of labour, the work was extremely slow and eventually it was to be another ten days before all the units of the Division were ashore.

The whole Turkish line, consisting of about 6,000 men, fell back on the 26 April and again on the following day, all about three miles. They created a new defensive line in a direction north west to south east in front of Krithia, from the area of Y Beach on the west coast to the high ground near Kereves Dere on the east coast. Four Turkish field batteries were in place near Krithia by the evening of 26 April, whilst a few forward posts were left to keep in touch with the British movements.

The men of the 29th Division near X Beach and W Beach spent a fairly quiet night on the 26 April. Patrols came back and reported that there were no enemy to be seen a mile from their front lines. However the overwrought troops near V Beach were edgy and could not sleep, fired their rifles at shadows and scrub and were too worn out to send out patrols. They therefore remained in ignorance of the Turkish withdrawal or the fact that the Turkish reinforcements were slow in arriving in the area. By the morning of the 27 there were only five Turkish battalions south of Achi Baba and only nine by nightfall.

27 APRIL 1915
On this day V beach was handed over to the French.
Major-General Hunter Weston was still resolute that Achi Baba had to be captured and the sooner the better. However, because of the delay in

V Beach, photographed 12 May, 1915. Taylor Library

the disembarkation of 2,000 soldiers of the French Metropolitan Brigade, which meant they would not be available until later that afternoon, he decided that the main attack would take place on April 28, twenty four hours later than intended. For the present he would order the 29th Division, together with the French battalions who would be under his tactical control for the present until General d'Amade's Headquarters could be established,

to advance at 4.00 pm and take up a line across the Peninsula from the high ground above S Beach to the mouth of Gully Ravine.

It was a lovely day as the 29th Division, together with the French 175th Regiment on the right, advanced across an apparently deserted Peninsula, thankfully meeting little opposition. By 5.30 pm the new line had been made, and the French had joined up with the men of the 2/SWB on S Beach. A problem existed, however, which was to have serious consequences. 87 Brigade had not advanced as far as intended, remaining in its original trenches to retain the good field of fire they enjoyed, and because of that the centre of the British front had to bend back sharply and face west, to link up with 87 Brigade.

By the evening of 27 April the Allies had secured a line, three miles long, extending from the west coast some 500 yards from the mouth of Gully Ravine to Eski Hissarlik Point (S Beach) in the east. The original landing beaches were now safe in the Allies hands.

And so the scene was set to continue for what was to become one of the most courageous, controversial and tragic campaigns in the First World War.

CASUALTIES

In summarising this aspect of the landings, we feel we should remember one of the many untold heroes involved on those fateful days. Captain Eric Stephenson DSO, Gloucestershire Regiment (attached Egyptian Army), an American, was appointed Landing Staff Officer on V Beach. He was mortally wounded on 26th April whilst assisting injured men, evacuated by the hospital ship Sicilia but died off the coast of Malta eleven days later. He was buried in Ta Braxia Cemetery, Malta

Total casualties for the 29th Division from the day of the Landings to evacuation amounted to 34,011. There were only 14 officers and 1,523 other ranks involved who landed at the start and were evacuated at the finish, without being invalided

(1) and (2)*Neill's Blue Caps* - H C Wylly
(3)VC's of the First World War Gallipoli - Snelling
(4) Dept. of Documents IWM

WALK NO 4 V BEACH

Starting Point: Krithia 6 kms. Sedd El Bahr 1km. Eceabat is 33 kms

It is recommended that you should begin your tour of the V Beach area at **Fort No.1 (Ertugrul) (1)** on the steep cliff top west of the village of Sedd El Bahr. This is easily reached from either the village itself or on leaving the Helles Memorial, following the road signposted. From Fort No. 1 a magnificent panorama of the V Beach area lies in front of you. Forming a natural amphitheatre, there are excellent views of V Beach itself, V Beach CWGC Cemetery, the Old Fort and Sedd El Bahr village, and the water tower and two cypress trees marking Hill 141 and the site of Lieutenant-Colonel Doughty-Wylie's grave. Views across the Straits to Kum Kale and Troy are also possible on a clear day and the Helles Memorial is behind you. Most important of all, one can still see where the SS *River Clyde* ran aground, along the second outcrop of rocks reaching into the sea and forming a low, narrow "pier".

Helm indicator from SS *River Clyde*.
The Royal Hampshire Regiment Museum

V Beach walk.

1. Fort No 1
2. Turkish Memorials
3. V Beach
4. V Beach Cemetery
5. Low Sandy Bank
6. SS *River Clyde*

7. Machine guns
8. Barbed wire
9. Trenches
10. Sedd El Bahr
11. Hill 141
12. Old Fort

13. The Camber
14. Northern Outskirts
15. Site of Lt Colonel Doughty-Wylie's grave

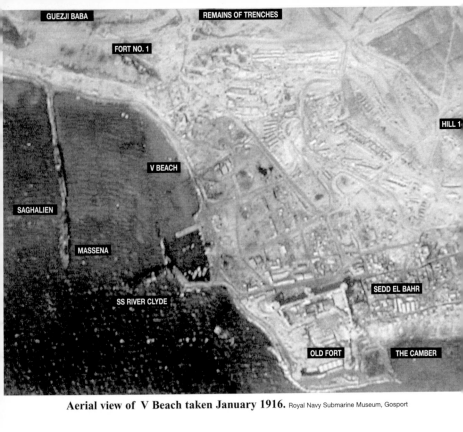

Aerial view of V Beach taken January 1916. Royal Navy Submarine Museum, Gosport

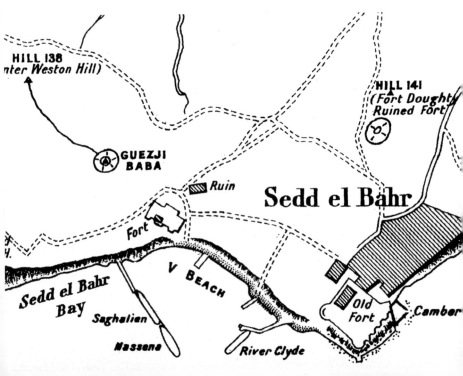

Fort No. 1 was one of the five gun emplacements which made up the Outer Defences of the Dardanelles, and the ramparts, the old ammunition bunkers and one of the 24 cm L/35 Krupp guns can still be seen. During the British naval actions of mid-February the fort was virtually demolished and it only played a very small role during the naval battle of 18 March 1915. The Fort was finally captured by the British on April 26.

In the vicinity of the Fort are **some Turkish memorials (2)** including a grave to Sehit (Private) Halil Ibrahim, apparently killed during an allied bombardment, although this appears to be fairly recent, but a monument with four panels, depicting the Turkish defence of V Beach by Sergeant Yahya and men of the 26 Regiment, was built in 1962. A symbolic cemetery has been made and there are some very recently reconstructed trenches.

There are several paths leading down to V Beach, the nearest being a rather steep, rocky track. Follow this towards the village, turning right after a few hundred metres, walking down to **the beach (3)**.

The modern houses, holiday homes, mosque, cafes and Mocamp Hotel now crawling along the low hills just above V Beach as the village of Sedd El Bahr has expanded need to be ignored.

With its far end almost in the sand , on your right hand side, will be found **V Beach Cemetery (4)**. It looks empty. It is sobering to learn that over five hundred men lie here, the majority in unnamed graves. There are just 20 named headstones, apart from special memorials.

V BEACH CWGC CEMETERY

This is a real battlefield cemetery, with the majority of those buried killed during the days immediately following the landings, including some eight officers of the Royal Dublin Fusiliers. Lieutenant Colonel Rooth (F 4) and the Reverend William Finn (F 4) lie next to each other. Captain Walford VC (O1) Major Grimshaw (F11) and Captain Ray (O17) all lie here, together with so many of their comrades.

Turn left and walk along the beach towards the Old Fort (Fort No 3) and note the **low sandy bank on your left (5)**, somewhat eroded but

V Beach cemetery.

still there, and recall how grateful the British troops must have been to at least have some shelter and respite from the lethal Turkish machine gun fire. Standing in the centre of the beach, facing out to sea, the SS *River Clyde*, with lighters forming a bridge, would have been on your left, by the **second outcrop of rocks (6)**. As the troops poured from the ship onto the gangplanks, they faced almost certain death from withering machine gun fire. The steam hopper, originally to form the link between ship and shore, would have lain broadside on, just in front of you, there also were the remains of the small boats, many filled with wounded troops and sinking slowly from holes made by machine gun bullets, bodies drifting in the blood-soaked water or immersed a few feet from the shore – such scenes would never be forgotten by those who survived that day. In this turquoise water the six Victoria Crosses were selflessly gained under the most appalling circumstances.

Turn to face inland and visualise the Turkish defences at V Beach. **Machine guns (7)** had been strategically placed to cover the whole of the landing area – on your left, one was close to the present site of V Beach cemetery, more guns some 200 yards inland from the centre of the beach, with at least one other machine gun in Fort No. 3. Whilst it was the accurate and persistent fire from these guns, as well as Turkish rifle fire and two pom poms, which caused most of the casualties, **other defences such as the solid barbed wire (8) and the carefully built trenches (9)** proved extremely difficult to break through to enable the quick capture of the **village of Sedd El Bahr (10)** and **Hill 141 (11)**. The strong rows of barbed wire, similar to that on W Beach, ran the length of the beach area from Fort No. 3 to the site of V Beach Cemetery. A hundred yards from the shore, Corporal Cosgrove, with his bare hands, had torn up great stakes covered with barbed wire and helped to make a breach inland for about 700 yards. There was more wire forming a barrier on the western edge of Sedd El Bahr village,

Sedd El Bahr village.

Krupp gun, No1 Fort.

running uphill towards Hill 141 and linking up with Guezji Baba (now the site of the Helles Memorial). With solid interlinking trenches, it is small wonder that the British troops found themselves pinned down for almost 36 hours.

Continue to walk towards the **Old Fort (12)**, eventually turning left in a northerly direction past its broken walls, where shell holes can still be seen. You are now in the vicinity of the extraordinarily courageous general advance on April 26, with the objectives of capturing this Fort, the village of Sedd El Bahr and Hill 141 itself, led by Lieutenant Colonel Doughty-Wylie, Captain Walford and Major Beckwith. It is possible admire the extensive views it must have enjoyed over the main entrance to the Dardanelles. In early 1915 it had ten large guns and a powerful searchlight, but because of naval attacks and Allied bombardments in February and March 1915, it did not offer a powerful threat on 25 April, other than as a machine gun emplacement. British troops eventually moving off V Beach found the main difficulty was fire from snipers carefully concealed in the ruins.

At the Old Fort are two Turkish memorials commemorating casualties from an Allied bombardment in November 1914, when a magazine was hit by a shell killing all outright and damaging the guns, some of which can still be seen. These are known as the Sedulbahir Ilk Sehitler Aniti near The Camber and the Seddulbahir (Cephanlik)

V beach.

Cemetery, a mass grave. Captured on 26 April, the Old Fort was soon occupied by the French, with General d'Amade making his headquarters there.

As you continue up into the village turn right at the end of the Fort and after 300 yards you will see a local café. At the rear is a pleasant terrace where you can sit with a cool drink and enjoy the excellent view of **The Camber (13)**, now a small fishing harbour, below, with Morto Bay, S Beach, De Tott's Battery and the massive Turkish Memorial in the distance. It is possible to walk down to The Camber, where the two platoons of 1/RDF landed under the cover of the cliffs, meeting strong opposition and losing all their officers. Just a very few managed to reach the village itself, and their bodies were found there the next day. Those who managed to return to the Camber were re-embarked by HMS *Queen Elizabeth*.

Make your way through the village to the large Mosque and continue to the junction with a bust of Kemal Attaturk.

Desperate house to house fighting took place in this area, a foothold was gained by 10.00 am on the 26th April and the exhausted troops managed to reach **the northern outskirts by midday (14)**.

Turn left and walk up the hill towards Hill 141. This is the direction taken by Lieutenant Colonel Doughty-Wylie and Major Grimshaw and where the men enthusiastically fixed bayonets and charged through the barbed wire and empty Turkish trenches to the summit.

Just after the sign to the Pansiyon Helles Panorama, turn right towards the two distinctive cypress trees and **the site of Lieutenant Colonel Doughty -Wylie's grave (15)**.

Surgeon Burroughes Kelly RN DSO wrote in his diary:

'Lieutenant Colonel Doughty-Wylie VC, Royal Welch Fusiliers
Early on the morning of the 26th, Doughty-Wylie left the River Clyde for the beach. He was prominent there throughout the forenoon, and about 11.00 am he returned and drank a cup of tea.

I had a chat of about of quarter of an hour with him, and he seemed depressed about the whole affair. Several times he remarked that something must be done. He then left us, and I recall vividly his walking-stick. The surviving troops had gradually got into Sedd El Bahr fort and up towards the main street of the village, and from where we were these places were well to the right of Hill 141, our objective. About 1.00 pm Doughty-Wylie placed himself at the head of the ever dwindling Dublins, Munsters and Hampshires, and waving his walking

Original grave on Hill 141 of Lt Col Doughty-Wylie VC CB CMG RWF.

stick and calling on the men to follow him, he led a gallant charge on the old fort at Hill 141. This charge carried the objective. As they entered, Doughty-Wylie, ever encouraging the men, fell to rise no more. He was shot through the head....Doughty-Wylie's last request was said to have been that someone bring to the notice of the authorities the "gallant Capt. Unwin and the boy Drewry". We buried him at midnight where he fell, and the River Clyde's carpenter made a simple wooden cross for his grave.

His close friend, Colonel Williams, wrote of finding Lieutenant Colonel Doughty-Wylie lying on the summit and continued:

I came up shortly after he had fallen; the men round about were full of admiration and sorrow. They told me he was first the whole way up the slope and it was only in the last few yards that some four or five men got up to and passed him actually over the castle walls; personally, I noticed him on two or three occasions always in front and cheering his men on.

As soon as I came up and realised that he was dead, I took his watch, money and a few things I could find and had him buried where he fell. I had this done at once, having seen such disgusting sights of unburied dead in the village that I could not bear to have him lying there.

The burial party worked quickly. A simple prayer was said and it was arranged that a temporary cross should be put in place to mark the spot.

Captain Guy Nightingale, 1/RMF, gave an moving eye witness

account, quoted in the Regimental History of the Royal Welch Fusiliers.

> *It was at this moment that Colonel Doughty-Wylie, who had led his men to the last moment, was killed by a shot in the head, dying almost immediately on the summit of the hill he had so ably captured. Colonel Doughty-Wylie was buried that evening by men of my company, and the Burial Service was read over his grave the following morning by our Regimental Chaplain, Father Harker, whom I had informed of the whereabouts of the grave.*
>
> *We left the hill that evening, and advanced a little, and I was not able to get an opportunity of visiting the scene for some six weeks. Later I found the grave in exactly the same place where I had seen him fall that day, and to which he had led his men from the moment he stepped off the SS River Clyde some eight hours before.*

The hill became known as Fort Doughty-Wylie.

Born at Theberton Hall, Suffolk into a well connected family, he was educated at Winchester and Sandhurst. Charles Doughty was gazetted into the Royal Welsh Fusiliers in September 1889 as a second lieutenant. He then served with great distinction in many far flung outposts of Empire. Conflicts such as the Nile Expedition, the Battle of Khartoum, the second Anglo Boer War (where he commanded a battalion of mounted infantry) meant he gained valuable experience. He acquitted himself well, was wounded twice and mentioned in despatches and was awarded an array of medals; by 1906 he had been promoted to Major.

He had married, in 1904, Lilian Adams in Bombay, and had assumed the additional name of Wylie by deed poll. In 1906 he decided to enter the realms of diplomacy and was appointed British Vice Consul in Konia, Turkey. He was in Adana when he witnessed the horrific massacre of some of the 22,000 Armenians. He could not stand by and let this happen, and with outstanding courage and leadership succeeded in outfacing the bloodthirsty mob and stopping the murders, afterwards organising relief for these destitute peoples.

It was during this period he met the archaeologist and writer Gertrude Bell, with whom he corresponded regularly and they became close friends. His skills as a diplomat did not go unseen and he was promoted Consul General in Addis Ababa until 1912, which saw the outbreak of the Balkan Wars. He was then appointed Director in Chief of Red Cross Units with the Turkish forces in Constantinople (Istanbul). Here his wife performed sterling work as Superintendent of Nursing Staff. (She continued to use her experience in nursing during the First World War, and was in charge of a hospital in St. Valery sur

Somme when the news of her husband's death arrived.)

Towards the end of 1913, after the conflict, his great experience was used to full effect when he was appointed President of the International Commission to establish the Albanian and Greek frontier. Promoted Lieutenant Colonel in 1913, when war broke out in August 1914 he was keen to return to active service. He joined Sir Ian Hamilton's GHQ on 18 March 1915 and was serving as Liaison Officer Intelligence when he was killed.

Lt Colonel C H H Doughty-Wylie's grave on Hill 141.

The grave remains in exactly the same place today, and is the only isolated battlefield grave on the Peninsula, with its commanding and magnificent views over Sedd El Bahr, V Beach, and the Straits, a fitting tribute to a gallant and steadfast hero, as Sir Ian Hamilton wrote in his eulogy. In the autumn of 1917 the solitary figure of a woman visited the site and laid a wreath - the only known female visitor to the Peninsula during the campaign. A certain mystery surrounds the visit, as it may have been Lilian Doughty-Wylie, or possibly Gertrude Bell, and it has been the subject of conjecture over the years. Permission for the visit was given by the French authorities, as the grave was in their area of responsibility, so perhaps the romantic streak in their personae is a clue!

His grave was left undisturbed until April 1923 when the Imperial War Graves Commission, who were then supervising the construction of the cemeteries on the Peninsula, arranged for an engineering

RWF past and present at the graveside of their regimental colleague.

company to rebuild the grave. The engineer in question, Mr. A. Cooke wrote:

> *The grave was located on a small knoll just outside the village. I was requested by the IWGC to make the site more permanent as his widow had in view building a monument over it. We went to the spot and I instructed my men to make a trench down to solid ground around it, then to pour concrete in it and to cap the whole grave with a 6 inch slab of concrete. ..Within a few inches his body became visible – enveloped in a ragged uniform with belt, huddled in a crouched position. ..I hurried to get the foundations around the bones and waited to put the concrete slab over him. I hope he now rests in peace.* [4]

No monument or cross apart from his headstone, was placed on the grave there, just two straight, tall pine trees, which prove very useful as they mark the summit of Hill 141 and assist with orientation.

During our regular visits to the Peninsula, individually or with

groups of friends, a pilgrimage is always made to that lonely grave, when his gallantry and courage is remembered. From time to time, we have been fortunate to have buglers serving with the present day 1/Royal Welch Fusiliers joining us, by kind permission of the Colonel. They proudly play their Regimental Quick March, The British Grenadiers, and it is always a moving moment when the strains of Last Post are heard across the hillside, now so peaceful, with the long grass rustling in the breeze. This concludes the walk and you can retrace your steps to Sedd El Bahr or Krithia.

In memory of the River Clyde

This nondescript collier has gone down in military folklore. The 4000-ton ship was built in Glasgow in 1905 and had been used to transport mules to North Africa. After the actual landing at V Beach the ship was used as a breakwater in the bay, an ammunition store, a field dressing station and for supplying fresh water. Indeed, in hindsight, it was an excellent addition to the task force. In 1919 the *River Clyde* was refloated and was bought by a Spanish shipping company. She sailed the Mediterranean until broken up in Spain in 1966.

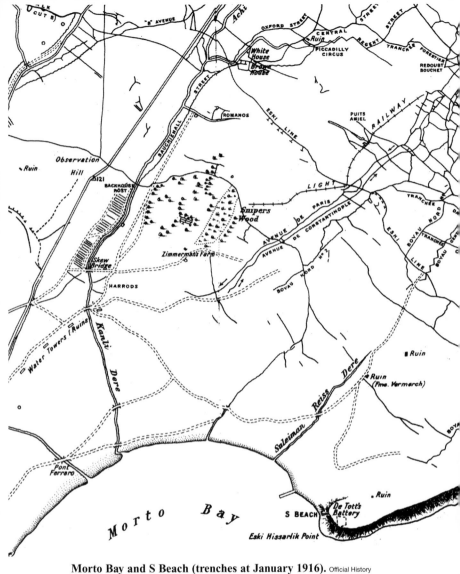

Morto Bay and S Beach (trenches at January 1916). Official History

A shady taverna overlooking Morto Bay.

Chapter Six

S BEACH – SUCCESS AT LAST

The *Daily Chronicle* of Wednesday July 7, 1915, contained reports from the 'Sunny South' of England:

Hove

Situated on the sunny side of a gentle slope of the South Downs, this fashionable seaside resort is now thronged with visitors,...Bathing from the beach and mixed bathing from tents is in full swing, and the golf courses, tennis courts, bowling greens etc. are excellent.

Littlehampton

The influx of visitors here is considerably above the average. Golf, boating and bathing are perhaps the favourite pastimes just now, but there are also excellent facilities for tennis, bowls and other summer games....

Published in the same edition is Sir Ian Hamilton's dispatch on the landings, reprinted from the London Gazette. Included is the following brief paragraph:

The detachment detailed for S Beach consisted of the 2nd South Wales Borderers (less one company) under Lieut. Colonel Casson. Their landing was delayed by the current, but at 7.30 am it had been successfully affected at the cost of some 50 casualties, and Lieut. Colonel Casson was able to establish his small force on the high ground near De Tott's Battery. Here he maintained himself until the general advance on April 27 brought him into touch with the main body.

Many a Welshman's interest in the Gallipoli Campaign of 1915 would focus on the landing of the 2/ South Wales Borderers on S Beach, or Morto Bay, as it is also called.

The bay is a lovely three mile stretch of concave shaped beach on the south west tip of the Gallipoli Peninsula, sheltered from the wind and with a backdrop of shady pine trees. As one enjoys a long, cool drink at the nearby taverna, the calm sea laps at the rusty remains of a sunken pier, and fishing boats putter to and fro. How different it must have been on 25 April 1915.

The landing on S Beach itself is defined as that point immediately in front of and around the old De Tott's Battery at the eastern end of Morto Bay, now the site of the commanding Turkish Memorial. This

Morto Bay and S Beach from De Tott's Battery.

landing was intended to be a diversionary action, along with that of the French at Kum Kale and Besika Bay and the stalwart efforts of the Royal Naval Division at Bulair,.

De Tott's Battery, situated on the cliff above the beach at Eski Hissarlik Point, originated from the Russo-Turkish War (1768 - 74). The construction of this artillery disposition had been supervised by one Baron Francois de Tott, a French artillery expert assisting the Ottoman Army.

From this position there is a superb view, with Asia clearly visible to the south, particularly of Kum Kale, the landing place of the French Army on 25 April 1915, and to the west the village of Sedd El Bahr and a little further the Helles Memorial to the Missing. Behind De Tott's Battery is the Turkish Memorial, cemetery, gardens and small museum.

On 25 April 1915 one of the objectives of the 29th Division was the capture of De Tott's Battery which, although in ruins, was used by the Turks as an observation post. This task was given specifically to the 2/ South Wales Borderers.

The Battalion arrived from the Far East on 12 January 1915, having been escorted part of the way by the Russian five funnelled cruiser *Askold,* known to the troops as the 'packet of Woodbines', and which they would see again during the Gallipoli landings. The Battalion dropped anchor in Plymouth Sound, before marching off to Coventry, where it joined 87 Brigade of the 29th Division.

The Battalion was refitted for service in France as well as being trained in methods of trench warfare to which the BEF had now been committed. The 2/SWB had had a taste of this type of warfare in

Tsingtao in the autumn of 1914, and it is of interest that the only other unit in the Division at this time which had recently fired a shot in anger was the famed L Battery, Royal Horse Artillery, reformed after its heroic stand at Nery during the Retreat from Mons.

Thus the 2/ SWB left England on 17 March 1915, the day before the second major naval battle in Gallipoli. They left Avonmouth on the SS *Canada* with 27 officers and 1,008 men, stopped at Mex Camp, Alexandria, for some days to re-equip, and then on to Mudros Harbour on the island of Lemnos, arriving there on 11 April. The Battalion Transport, following in the *Manitou,* narrowly escaped destruction by an attack by a Turkish torpedo boat off Skyros. Fortunately all three torpedoes failed to hit their target, but not before the order was given to abandon ship. Most of the men were picked up by British destroyers, but some fifty men were drowned.

The 2/ SWB now prepared for their diversionary attack at S Beach. The plan was that HMS *Cornwallis* should proceed two and half miles inside the Straits when the troops would be transferred to four trawlers. Each trawler would tow six small boats, three on either side, a total of 24 small boats altogether, with about 34 men to each boat.

Because the Navy's resources were limited, only three companies of the Battalion could be deployed at S Beach; hence A Company, under Captain Palmer, was detached and was added to the two battalions detailed for Y Beach.

The SS *Alaunia* steamed out of Mudros Harbour carrying the main body of the 2/SWB on 23 April. As she passed HMS *Triumph,* the Battalion's escort on the China station and at Tsingtao, the ship's band struck up Men of Harlech, which of course brought a rousing reception from the Welshmen. They arrived at Tenedos early on 24 April, when the Battalion transferred in the afternoon to HMS *Cornwallis*, where they were warmly welcomed and, after a good meal, tried to get some rest.

At 10.00 pm the ship weighed anchor and began to steam slowly towards the south of the Gallipoli Peninsula. At 03.30 am on the 25 April she reached her assigned position station, west of Tekke Burnu. The men of 2/SWB were awakened and given breakfast.

As can be seen from the following extract from *A Memorandum for the information and guidance of all concerned regarding the landing of D C and B Companies, 24 Regiment, and details attached, at Beach S*, signed by Lieutenant Colonel H.G.Casson, meticulous attention to detail had been involved in the planning for this landing and very precise arrangements made. For example, the boats on either side of each trawler would be numbered with even numbers on the port (left) side and odd numbers on the starboard (right) side. Each boat had its own particular designated landing place on the beach.

Distribution of landing force by trawlers and boats to beach is as follows:

(a) Trawler No. 362 is allotted to D Company, 24 Regiment
Each boat to contain 34 officers and men D Company 1 man RE and 1 naval rating - Total per boat = 36. Total 216

In the notes that followed the Commanding Officer emphasised that all officers and men would be 'detailed by name to their respective boats' and would be told where to sit in that boat. He stressed that,

absolute silence is to be maintained in each boat under any circumstances, and all are to sit still unless ordered by the officer or NCO in charge to move.

In case of casualties, individually named spare rowers were to be told to sit near the original rowers ready to take their places immediately if needed.

Included in the equipment were rifles, wire cutters, picks and shovels, boxes of ammunition and cases of water. All the men of C and B Companies were also to wear their packs. As their orders were to land on the eastern side of the beach and scale the cliffs, D Company's packs were to be wrapped in waterproof sheets and stowed in the boats.

The total number of men landing would be in excess of 800. The young officer in charge of No. 13 Platoon D Company wrote in his diary that there was a 'lovely sunrise' that morning.

As they were transferred to their trawlers they heard the roar of the guns and the screech of shells as the warships started their bombardment of the mainland at about 5.00 am. The four trawlers edged their way towards the coast but had quite a difficult time, owing to strong tides and mine sweeping flotillas inside the Straits, which caused a frustrating delay, especially as the landings were supposed to take place simultaneously at X, W, Y and S Beaches.

At about 6.30 am the flagship signalled to them to avoid S Beach and make for V Beach, but fortunately for the men this signal was not seen and the trawlers held their course across Morto Bay, making for S Beach. Just as the trawlers reached shallower water and they started to transfer to the small boats, the men saw the Russian 'Packet of Woodbines' (*Askold*) cruising on the Asiatic side firing her broadsides. The trawlers let their tows loose, and the troops pulled hard on their oars and stealthily grounded their little boats at about 7.30 am, leaping into the waist-deep water and moving to the shore as quickly as they could.

An extract from the 2/SWB War Diary for that day records baldly:

7.00 am made signal for men to enter small boats.

7.30 am Landing effected as follows.

Trawlers in succession steamed in towards shore, on getting in as close as possible a storm anchor was thrown out and small boats cast away. These boats rowed for the shore as quickly as possible.

D Company 1st to land made for De Tott's Battery at once, C&B Coys on landing made for trench in front of beach at a range of about 100 yds.

Manoeuvre completely successful.

8.30 Our position secured.

D Company under Major Margesson were the first to arrive, landing

Extract from Lieutenant. Colonel Casson's memo for the S Beach landing.

(VII) Absolute silence is to be maintained in each boat under any circumstances and all are to sit still unless ordered by the Officer or N.C.O in charge of boats.

(VIII) No alteration is to be made in the distribution of men, etc, to boats without reference to the O.C, e.g. if a man is for any reason unable to disembark he merely drops out of his particular boat.

(IX) It is essential that every Officer and man should at once be told which is his Trawler and boat, and where he is to sit in the latter.

5/ General instructions re action to be taken on landing will be issued to all concerned.

H.G. Casson Lt Colonel

S.S "Alaunia"
23rd April 1915   Commanding 2nd South Wales Borderers

on the rocks immediately below De Tott's Battery. B and C Companies landed on S Beach shortly after, further to the left, with the Commanding Officer, Lieutenant Colonel Casson, and the Captain of HMS *Cornwallis*, Captain A Davidson, who insisted on landing personally. The soldiers were also supported by a small detachment of 30 engineers, a party of 21 medics with stretchers, an artillery liaison officer and signallers, together with a group of marines and naval ratings serving aboard HMS *Cornwallis*. There were some casualties, including 21 year old Lieutenant Behrens, who was mortally wounded. He was buried at sea and is commemorated on the Helles Memorial.

This area of the Peninsula fortunately had few defences. Unlike W and V Beaches, there was no wire. One platoon of the 2/26 Regiment guarded the position, with a second platoon about half a mile further inland.

D Company were in shirtsleeve order. Unhampered by packs, they quickly scaled the cliff which appeared to rise straight up to about two hundred feet. According to one of the 13 Platoon officers, making for the top of the cliff proved quite difficult,

> *for our putties and trousers were wet through and although we are under cover from enemy fire, the shells from the Fleet are still bursting on top of the cliff, the falling stones etc causing several minor casualties.*

Near the top the men gathered themselves for a final effort to fling themselves over the summit.

They ran towards the ruins of the battery, approaching it from both sides. These ruins consisted of the outer walls, which were at right angles to each other, and formed two sides of a square. The one running north for about one hundred yards varied in height from between eight feet to twelve feet, whilst the other, which ran west towards S Beach for about one hundred yards, was lower, being

The approach to S Beach today.

between two and eight feet. The troops immediately captured these and soon turned them into defensive positions, with loopholes for firing, and were able to enfilade the Turkish trenches facing the bay.

A party of Marines soon followed D Company up the cliff and later spoke admiringly of the Welshmen setting to work to defend the position, putting snipers in strategic places and ensuring that a telephone line was run down the cliff in order that communications could be maintained. Fierce fire from a nearby Turkish position poured down on B and C Companies, who were still on the beach, but this was soon dealt with by D Company. Many of the Turks ran away, whilst others were shot and bayoneted, with about a dozen being taken prisoner.

The cliff climbed by D. Coy 2/SWB.

An account from D Company reads:

Sunday 25 April

Reveille 3.30 am. Got a swill and breakfast at 4.00 am and paraded at 4.30 and got to the Sweeper 362 which towed three boats on each side. My platoon, No. 1 boat starboard side. Sweeper steamed in as close as possible. Full fire from the forts. They were fairly good shots and missed our boat by inches several times, but we got away scot-free. As soon as the sweeper was as far in as possible, we took to the rowing boats. We were second boat off, our lads pulled with a will and we beached at the extreme end of Hill 236 at 7.30 am. The lads hopped out quick and we had an upright cliff to climb...there we found a trench wall running north to south along the top for about one hundred yards and then bearing south for 100 yards. So as it was too high to fire over, we went along under cover to the bend where we saw a breach. Here Major Margesson, who was following me, went out into the open and must have been immediately shot down, although we did not move him for some time.[1]

The death of 44 year old Major Margesson, who was shot in the chest, and died within the hour, proved a great loss. Lieutenant Blake of the

Remains of De Tott's battery with Turkish memorial in the background. Major Margesson 2/SWB fell close by.

RAMC was unable to do anything for him. He was buried in the evening on top of the cliff at the entrance to the Dardanelles, about three yards from the wall of D Tott's Battery. It is sad to record that his body was never recovered after the end of the First World War, so his name is today recorded on the Helles Memorial to the Missing.

From his home in Worthing, Sussex he went on to serve in the Regular Army from 1891 and had seen conflict in Central Africa, served in the Ashanti wars, Somaliland and Southern Nigeria. Together with Lieutenant Colonel Casson, he was mentioned in despatches for the second time for his work under very trying conditions in Tsingtao, China

In the Brecon County Times in July 1915, an article entitled, *2nd SWB in Gallipoli – Heroic Performance of Hazardous Work* and based on the book *The Immortal Gamble* by Commander Steward RN and the Rev C Peshall, Chaplain RN, gives a 'thrilling account by eye-witnesses' of the actions of 2/SWB on 25 April 1915:

That evening the Cornwallis *left the Tenedos anchorage and steamed towards the Gallipoli Peninsula. At 3.30 am on the morning of the 25th trawlers came along side and loaded up with our soldier guests. It was a lovely morning, cold and windless, with a calm glassy sea, and presently the sun came up in a flood of gold - the last sunrise many of us were destined to look upon. Silently we steamed up the Straits in grey light, and ahead of us crept the soldier-filled trawlers, until we anchored short of De Tott's Battery.*

When the water shoaled up and the trawlers could go no closer, the boats were cast off to pull themselves ashore. Many of them, of course, had never handled an oar before, but somehow or other they accomplished the feat of grounding the boat a few yards from the land, which as it then appeared might have been a desert island...

Into the water up to their middles the soldiers jumped, and a

hot rifle fire was opened on them as they dashed ashore and, without a moment's hesitation, made for the two arranged points of attack - the steep cliff and the slope on the left. It was an unforgettable experience to watch this well trained battalion working its way methodically and without confusion to the top of the battery from both sides.

By about 8.00 am, just half an hour later, all the careful planning had had its reward. The 2/SWB had achieved their objective and S Beach had been secured. It was time to consolidate, arrange for the wounded to be taken to the ship, and manhandle the boxes of ammunition and cases of water out of the small boats. This proved not to be straightforward as some of these boats were now drifting on the open sea and the naval ratings, instead of making them secure, in their enthusiasm had joined in the general charge up the beach on landing, stopping to grab a rifle from the early casualties.

Lieutenant Colonel Casson now had to plan his next move. His men were now being fired upon from the Asiatic shore, he could hear the sound of continuous shelling by the British fleet on Sedd El Bahr and there was also heavy firing from the vicinity of V Beach. It seemed quite apparent that the troops on V Beach were not yet in any position to make an immediate advance.

Despite the distance involved and the consequent inaccuracy, there were also machine guns at Sedd El Bahr endeavouring to fire in the rear of B and C Companies and also from enemy snipers on Hill 236, a feature some 500 yards to the north. There would be the possibility of a counter attack, and possible danger from 2000 Turkish reinforcement troops reported by a Turkish prisoner, although it transpired later that, whilst these did exist, they were not in the vicinity

Reproduced by Survey Dept., Egypt – scale 1:40,000. Note Hill 236 and De Tott's Battery.

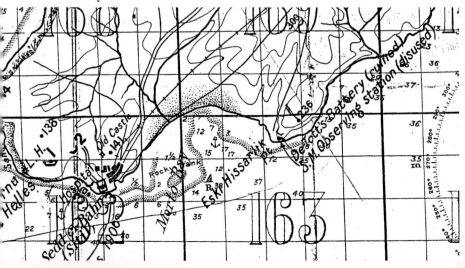

of S Beach. 2/SWB were not to know that only some 200 Turks were in their immediate locality.

The *2/SWB War Diary* makes the point:

9.00 am Watched for landing at Sedd El Bahr. This however did not appear to be a success, we could see troops trying to work up through the ruined village but without success.

10.00 am Troops observed moving from X Beach moving East. This attack however appeared to be diverted towards Sedd El Bahr. From this fact we gathered that the landing at Sedd El Bahr had failed and we were quite isolated.

In view of all these considerations, Lieutenant Colonel Casson made the decision that the 2/SWB should dig in and be ready to resist any counter attack. This was in line with the instructions he had been given before the landings, that after the beaches at Y and S had been captured, the commanders were to await the advance from the south, and then to join in the attack on Achi Baba. It appeared that no apparent thought had been given to the possibility that, after successful landings at Y and S, these troops could then give assistance to those at X, W and V Beaches.

He then disposed the men accordingly. According to *The History of the South Wales Borderers* by Captain Atkinson:

D Company and a platoon of C held De Tott's, three platoons of B and half one of C formed the front line along a ridge facing North, the rest of B and C being in support nearer the beach, while a field hospital was established just below De Tott's in some trees, where an excellent supply of water was found. A sharp watch was kept on the Sedd El Bahr-Cape Helles area.

The Commanding Officer's decision was confirmed by 29th Division HQ, but really there did not appear to be any alternative.

Whilst it could be said that no advantage was taken of the success of this landing on the eastern flank of the Peninsula, the remainder of the 29th Division was over two miles away, heavily engaged and suffering severe casualties. Even if this contingency had been considered and prepared for, it would possibly have been foolish to ask three companies of infantry to advance further inland, unsupported and with little likelihood of immediate reinforcement.

Later, in his diary, General Sir Ian Hamilton stated that he was afraid to risk the troops on Y Beach and S Beach in a pincer movement around the rear of Sedd El Bahr, but then he was completely unaware that the troops on these two beaches at the time of landing were collectively greater than the whole Turkish force south of Achi Baba.

The total casualties according to the 2/SWB War Diary on S Beach that morning were two officers, Major Margesson killed and Lieutenant Behrens died of wounds and buried at sea, 12 men killed and three officers (Captain D. G. Johnson, Captain Birkett and Lieutenant Chamberlain) wounded together with 40 other ranks, with six missing.

Captain Dudley Graham Johnson, who in October 1918 was awarded the Victoria Cross for actions on the Sambre Canal whilst commanding the Royal Sussex Regiment, just yards south of where Wilfred Owen, poet and soldier, had been killed earlier that day, was born in Gloucestershire in 1884. He was commissioned into the 2/South Wales Borderers in 1903 and in October 1912 he accompanied 2/SWB as part of the International Force of the North China Command and at the action at Tsingtao in 1914, as a captain, he was awarded the DSO and also Mentioned in Despatches.

After his wounds on 25 April he was invalided back to the UK where he served until returning to France in 1917. Initially commanding 1/SWB in early 1918, he was then attached to the 2/Royal Sussex Regiment, where he showed such wonderful courage and leadership during the crossing of the Sambre Canal.

On 14 June 1919 he was decorated with the Victoria Cross by HM King George V at Buckingham Palace, at the same time receiving the Bar to his DSO for his actions at Pontruet, 1918 and the Military Cross. He was ADC to HM King George VI from 1936 - 1939. When the Second World War broke out, he was GOC 4th Division, and was present at the evacuation of the BEF from Dunkirk.

He retired in 1944 after 41 years of service at the age of 60 – a greatly respected soldier and inspirational leader.

At the Presentation of the Freedom of the Borough of Newport to the *Corps of the South Wales Borderers* on Friday 23 May 1947 the Colonel of the Regiment was Major General D.G. Johnson VC, CB, DSO, MC. He died in 1975 and is buried in Church Crookham Cemetery, Church Crookham, Hampshire.

It became apparent during the night of 25/26 April that the Turkish positions were along a ridge about 800 – 1,000 yards away, from where spasmodic bursts of heavy rifle fire came. Patrols from 2/SWB were sent out, but for the most part the men tried to get some fitful rest. A patrol from B Company brought in two Turkish prisoners. The main excitement that night was the welcome arrival of more rations and extra ammunition, which were stacked under the cliff.

Daylight on 26 April brought little change. The troops attempted to improve their defences and hold their position. The 2/SWB War Diary states that most of the morning was spent in attempting to direct the fire of ships onto the Turks, who were retiring from the direction of the village of Sedd El Bahr. They were heartened by a message from Major General Hunter Weston with the words, 'Well done, SWB. Can you maintain your position for another 48 hours?'

They were also greatly cheered when they realised, during the middle of the afternoon, that V Beach, the village of Sedd El Bahr and Hill 141 had been taken at last. There was, however, still no sign of a general advance by those exhausted troops to link up with S Beach itself.

Night came once again and once again patrols were sent out. The troops had to face some sniping by the enemy, but there was no attack made. A note in their War Diary for this period mentions that,

> appearances point to the fact that the Turks are rather afraid
> of us, they prefer to remain at a distance and snipe.

The men stood to arms most of the night, alert to any attempt to drive them back into the sea – it was a tense and nerve racking time.

The morning of 27 April was also very quiet and it was not until later that day that Lieutenant Colonel Casson was advised that French troops, in the form of three battalions of the 175th Regiment, would relieve his men, who were to march across the Peninsula and rejoin its own 87 Brigade, which was now taking over the left of the 29th Division's line. This was a distance of some four miles of unknown and rough terrain. However it was 7.00 pm when the first two French battalions arrived at De Tott's battery. *The History of the South Wales Borderers* records:

> Their Colonel was very anxious for Colonel Casson to remain
> for the night to assist his battalion in securing the position, and
> it was well after midnight before, the taking over being
> completed, the SWB moved off towards X Beach.

Some of the Frenchmen spoke English, so it was not too difficult for the relief to be accomplished efficiently.

Having marched wearily across the dark, scrub-covered and difficult countryside, with the noise of jackals in their ears and the sight of many dead Turkish soldiers, on reaching X Beach at 5.30 am the Regiment were in for a shock. 2/SWB were ordered to be ready for the general advance to Achi Baba at 8.00 am on that same morning from Gully Ravine.

This Welsh battalion thereafter remained on the Peninsula and were present in actions in such places as The Boomerang, Suvla,

Damakjelik Bair, Scimitar Hill and Hill 60, all of which have gone into the annals of military history. The men of the SWB fought in these actions with distinction and great courage – but that is another story.

This part of the South Wales Borderers' story would not be complete without mention of the then Commanding Officer, Lieutenant Colonel Casson. At the outbreak of the First World War he was Commanding Officer of 2/South Wales Borderers in Tientsin, China. He led his men ably in trying conditions at Tsingtao after which General Barnardiston, GOC British troops in the North China Command, warmly recommended the Regiment to the GOC of the 29th Division declaring,

> that he had nothing but the highest praise for the 2/South Wales Borderers and that their new commanders were lucky to have them under them.

Having led his men with great ability, in further fighting in May 1915, during the Second Battle of Krithia, Colonel Casson found himself temporarily commanding a brigade of the Royal Naval Division on May 7, resuming command of his own men on 11 May. 87 Brigade was again commanded by Colonel Casson during the Third Battle of Krithia on 4 June. It was a sad day for the men of the 2/SWB when in mid-July 1915 Colonel Casson was appointed to the command of the Scots of 157 Brigade, 52nd Division, which was then on the Peninsula. They would miss his caring attitude and concern for their welfare, his thoroughness, and his meticulous attention to detail in trying to avoid unnecessary casualties. Brigadier General HG Casson CB survived the Great War. He had had a very distinguished military career, having been Mentioned in Despatches five times.

However, it is also pertinent to mention that amongst 2/SWB in Gallipoli was 8206 Company Sergeant Major Sidney Davis Bean from Tiverton, Somerset, who had enlisted in the Regular Army in 1903. A dashing figure with his blue eyes, brown hair, and fresh complexion, he had proved himself a very reliable and efficient soldier. In a renewed attack at 5.30 pm on 8 May on Fir Tree Spur, during the battle that raged at Krithia, when the advance was held up about one hundred yards from the Turkish position, he saw two of his young officers had fallen in the hail of machine gun fire. Taking stock of the situation, he realised he was the most senior man present, and immediately took charge, telling the men to take cover and hold their position. As *The History of the South Wales Borderers* states:

> His fine example of courage and steadiness was ably seconded by Lance Corporal Millward, who ran up and down the

Citation for CSM S D Bean.

line with orders, seeming to bear a charmed life.

On 13 May General Hunter Weston visited the battalion, now with a strength of only about 500, and warmly congratulated them on their 'splendid conduct in the recent severe fighting'. For his actions, together with Lance Corporal Millward and three other Privates, CSM Bean was awarded the DCM. The citation reads:

No 8206 Sgt Bean 2/South Wales Borderer, who, on the evening of 8 May when all the officers of C and D Companies in the firing line had been either killed or wounded, took charge, making the men lie still under a very heavy machine gun fire, and after dusk, brought back to safety all that remained of these two companies in the firing line. This NCO by his steady example maintained the line in front, although it was under an exceptionally heavy fire and undoubtedly saved many lives as any man who moved at all was at once shot down.

Later in the campaign he was wounded and invalided to the UK. In 1927 the Adjutant of 2/SWB was to write an Assessment Report for the now RSM Bean:

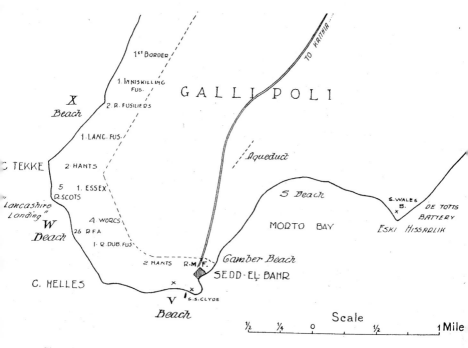

Situation of 29th Division – 26 April, 1915. Essex Regimental Museum, Chelmsford

> *A really good type of Warrant Officer. Commands the respect of all ranks. He is intelligent, honest and strictly sober. Entirely trustworthy and energetic...He is a good instructor and takes a passionate interest in sport. Great sense of organisation and entirely reliable.*

It could be said that men like him were indeed the backbone of the British Regular Army.

WALK NO 5 S BEACH

Starting Points: *a) Krithia (7kms) b) Sedd El Bahr (2.5kms)*
Eceabat is 28 kms from S Beach.
Time allowed: Two - Two and a half hours

a) If approaching Morto Bay from Krithia along the Krithia Road, you will pass **Skew Bridge Cemetery (1)**, about 1.5 kms from Sedd El Bahr. Turn left at the signpost to Cannakale Sehitligi and follow the road past the Abide Motel to **the beach (2)**, a distance of about 1500 yards.
b) If travelling from Sedd El Bahr, continue out of the village on the main road to Krithia for a few hundred metres. Turn right at the junction signposted to Cannakale Sehitligi and follow the same route as above.

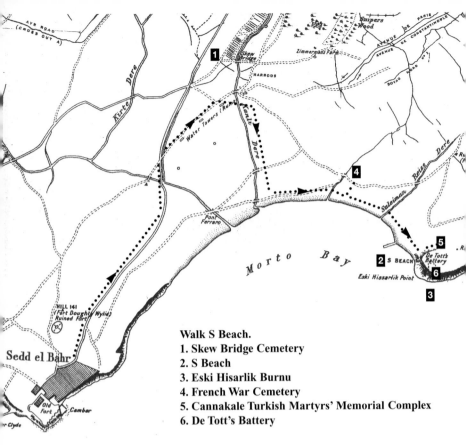

Walk S Beach.
1. Skew Bridge Cemetery
2. S Beach
3. Eski Hisarlik Burnu
4. French War Cemetery
5. Cannakale Turkish Martyrs' Memorial Complex
6. De Tott's Battery

Sheltered **Morto Bay /S Beach (2)** begins NE of the village of Sedd El Bahr and follows a wide semi circle of nearly three kilometres until it reaches the headland known as **Fortress Point or Eski Hisarlik Burnu (3)**. S Beach is in an attractive setting and a good place to swim. In the group of shady pine trees there is a picnic area, parking and a local taverna with drinks and food available on the opposite side of the road. The friendly dogs are a bonus - if you like dogs!

The main points of interest in this area are **S Beach** itself, the **French War Cemetery (4)** a little further on and the complex at the **Cannakale Turkish Martyrs' Memorial (5)**.

The names of three deres (streams) that run into the Bay – Kirte Dere, Kanli Dere and Suleiman Reiss Dere – would have become well known to the men of the British Army in the ensuing battles to try and capture Krithia and Achi Baba.

From the taverna on the left hand side cross over on to S Beach and note the remains of a **French-built pier**. To the east the cliffs jut out into the bay, on top of which is the **Cannakale Turkish Martyrs**

Remains of French pier S Beach.

Memorial.

The Turks had very few defences here, in stark comparison to W and V Beaches, and there was no barbed wire. One platoon had been ordered to man some trenches on the slopes of the open beach.

The steep cliffs, now covered with scrub and grass, had been quickly climbed by D Company 2/SWB in their shirt sleeves, under the command of Major Margesson, after landing on the rocks immediately below and to the east of the headland. It is not recommended that you climb the cliffs, so return to the main road, and proceed back along the coast road for a short distance to the sign for the **French Cemetery**. Continue up the path towards a parking area.

FRENCH WAR CEMETERY and MEMORIAL (4)

Overlooking Morto Bay, with its bare black metal crosses, its striking white tower, and well tended and distinctive rosemary bushes. the cemetery commemorates 3,216 burials, with four ossuaries at the rear of the Cemetery, each containing the remains of 3,000 unknown soldiers. The main obelisk is also an ossuary. The various memorial plaques include sailors who died in submarines and there is a special memorial tablet to the French battleship *Bouvet*, sunk on 18 March during the Allied naval attack.

Continue uphill for a further 1300 metres to the vast Turkish Memorial complex, passing a French gun on the left hand side. For the present turn right and walk past the Turkish Cemetery and memorial park to **the edge of the cliffs where you will find strewn around the point what are the foundations of what was known as De Tott's**

183

The impressive French Cemetery.

Battery(6), from where on a clear day outstanding views can be had of S Beach, west to Sedd El Bahr, the Camber and Helles Memorial and south across the straits to Asia and Kum Kale. A French report noted that it was

> *now only ruins, stones, with just a bit of wall which enables*
> *one to judge the importance of the buildings.*

It was used as an observation post by the Turks in 1915.

As previously mentioned, D Company 2/SWB successfully captured these ruins and turned them into defensive positions. From here they would have seen their comrades of B and C Companies packed together in the small boats approaching the beach, landing and then charging towards the Turkish trenches. Major Margesson was killed at the moment of victory, close to one of the ruined walls of the Battery and was buried that same evening where he fell, and there he remains. The landing had been a great success, with comparatively few casualties and went completely to plan. The French took over this position two days later and during the campaign held the area here and to the north, extending to a radius of about four kilometres, with two divisions, although by August the troops were severely reduced by sickness and a high casualty rate.

Return to the **Turkish memorial complex (5)** which includes the huge **Cannakale Turkish Martyrs' Memorial** (completed in 1960 and built of concrete pylons, with a flat roof, 40 metres high) where the official National Turkish ceremonies are held each year, often attended by the Turkish President; a small Museum of battlefield artefacts is open daily, with snack bar and wc; a Memorial garden; several groups of statues, the most important of which is of Kemal Attaturk gazing over the battlefield; and an attractive symbolic cemetery commemorating 100 officers and 500 men who died during the campaign and who came from each province of the Ottoman Empire. But perhaps the most moving is the Memorial Wall, with many names of the missing soldiers of the Turkish nation.

From here return to your starting point.

Chapter Seven

FEINT ATTACKS

The plan for the landings included diversionary actions in three separate locations – Kum Kale, Besika Bay and Bulair.

At **Kum Kale** the French force of 2,800 landed successfully on a small beach immediately under the fort at Kum Kale after a bombardment by the French Navy on the villages of Kum Kale, Orhanie and Yeni Shehr. However, after slowly consolidating the position with little opposition, the French had to face four determined Turkish counter attacks during the night of 25/26 April and both sides suffered severe casualties. By the evening of 26 April the French had been evacuated from Kum Kale to V Beach, having lost 778 men in this diversion. The Turkish losses amounted to approximately 1,750, including some 500 missing.

The French Navy also made a small demonstration early in the morning on 26 April in **Besika Bay**, 8 miles south of

A French soldier's sketch of Gallipoli Peninsula. Mme, Stocanne

Kum Kale Fort.

Feint attacks Bulair.

Kum Kale, in order to confuse the enemy and ensure some Turkish troops remained in the area. Ten ships were involved. The surrounding beaches were blasted with shells and small boats lowered to simulate landings. At 10.00 am the ships sailed to Tenedos.

The Royal Naval Division carried out a further successful diversion in the area of **Bulair** in the Gulf of Saros on 25 April. The Bulair Lines, reaching across the narrow neck of land on the northern end of the Peninsula, were relics of Anglo French defences dating from the Crimean War 1854/56. From early morning both HMS *Dartmouth* and HMS *Doris* carried out a bombardment over the Bulair lines which

186

went on all day and boats were lowered to simulate troop landings. In the evening, Lieutenant Commander Freyburg, an International swimmer of some repute, volunteered to swim, naked and covered in black grease, in freezing cold waters, to the shore to light flares and generally cause confusion. Two Turkish divisions were kept in this position for almost two days as result of his efforts, for which he was awarded the DSO. After this the RND sailed south to join the main landing forces.

Lieutenant Commander B C Freyburg.

AFTERTHOUGHT

No amount of research or walking the ground can really put this campaign into perspective. There are probably no survivors left today who can remember or know what actually happened, and as for the rest of us, we can only surmise and try to imagine the appalling difficulties, the hardships and quite frankly the impossibility of what the men were trying to achieve. As far as we are concerned we can only stand on the beaches and thank all those brave lads who landed there in 1915. They did all that was asked of them and could have done no more. Whilst the campaign is generally regarded today as a resounding military and naval defeat for the Allies, the spirit of those who fought was not defeated.

The total British casualty figures for the period 25 - 30 April 1915, as stated in the Official History, amounted to 187 Officers and 4,266 Other Ranks. The strength of the three Brigades of the 29th Division on 1 May 1915 was 149 Officers and 6,746 men. Compare this with a normal Divisional strength at that time of approximately 15000 and one can appreciate the severe losses incurred.

As many visitors and pilgrims to the Gallipoli Peninsula, including the authors, may attest, the following lines from Ernest Raymond's contemporary novel *Tell England*, expressing the feelings of his two heroes on leaving the battlefield for the last time, whilst a touch whimsical – some might even say sentimental – strike a note of empathy:

On the Redbreast *we leaned upon the rail, looking back. The boat began to steam away, and Monty,*

Ernest Raymond soldier and writer.

187

knowing with whom the thoughts of both of us lay, said quietly:
'Tell England' – you must write a book and tell 'em, Rupert,
about the dead schoolboys of your generation –
Tell England, ye who pass this monument,
We died for her, and here we rest content.

Unable to conquer a slight warming of the eyes at these
words, I watched the Peninsula pass. All that I could see of it in
the moonlight was the white surf on the beach, the slope of
Hunter Weston Hill, and the outline of Achi Baba, rising behind
like a monument.

Those who visit the Gallipoli Peninsula find it still exerts a compelling and powerful fascination for what happened there in 1915 but nowhere more so than on the beaches. Perhaps it begins with the terrible tragedy of some of the landings which burns into their spirit and touches their hearts.

Orlo Williams, Chief Cypher Officer, wrote:

A wonder; yes. That is the word for those days. The scenes, the
men, the actions, the great ships, the smell of thyme mixed with
the reek of cordite, the knowledge that immortal history has been
made before one's eyes. I do not praise War, but there I saw deeds
rise fully to the heights of a great issue, in a noble setting, giving
a quality to those days, with all their suffering, that aeons of grey
evolution can hardly attain.

WE MUST NEVER FORGET

SELECTED BIBLIOGRAPHY/RECOMMENDED FURTHER READING

History of the Great War - Military Operations Gallipoli Vols.1 and 2
Brigadier General C F Aspinall-Oglander

Official Hisotry of Australia in the War of 1914-1918
The Story of Anzac Vols. 1 and 2

Various Regimental Histories including those of the following:

1/Lancashire Fusiliers	1/Royal Munster Fusiliers
1/Kings Own Scottish Borderers	1/Royal Dublin Fusiliers
1/Border Regiment	4/Worcestershire Regiment
2/Royal Fusiliers	1/Essex Regiment
1/Royal Inniskilling Fusiliers	2/Hampshire Regiment
Plymouth Battalion Royal Marine	1/Royal Welch Fusiliers
Light Infantry	2/South Wales Borderers

Neill's Blue Caps Volume 3. Colonel H C Wylly

Gallipoli Robert Rhodes James

Gallipoli Memories Compton McKenzie

To What End did they Die? R W Walker

Gallipoli John Masefield

Dardanelles Commission Report

From Trench and Turret S M Holloway

Corbett Naval History

Times History of the Great War Volumes 4 and 5

Deeds That Thrill the Empire

VCs of the Great War - Gallipoli
Stephen Snelling

The Hood Battalion
Douglas Jerrold

The Victoria Cross 1856 - 1920 Sir O'Moore Creagh

Hell's Foundations Geoffrey Moorhouse

Verses Letters and Remembrances of Sub. Lieutenant A Waldern St Clair Tisdall VC Naval & Military Press

The Secret Battle Aubrey Herbert

History of the Great War John Buchan

Winston Churchill and the Dardanelles T Higgins

Gallipoli - A Battlefield Guide Phil Taylor and Pam Cuper

Gallipoli Major and Mrs. T Holt

SELECTIVE INDEX

Abershon Captain 53
Adams Major 84,92
Addison Captain 145,146
Allenby General E 29
Aspinall Major 42
Bartholomew Lt WG 71,73

Beaches:
  Y   21,38, **43-59**,70,74,75,123,151,169,170,176
  Gully 22,47
  X 21,22,38,42,43,45,47,48,50, **64-76**,81,90,93,95,
        99,123,128,144,159,170,176,178
  Bakery 22
  W 22,38,40,42,45,48,59,67,70, **80-109**, 120,
      123,128,141,143,144,145,150,170,172,176
  V 6,17,23,38,42,45,48,70,81,84,92,95,98,
      99,**119-154**,170,172,175,176
  S **24,43,45,52,58,59,70,75,123,128,154,164-**
     181,177
Bean CSM SD 179,180
Beatty Admiral 42
Beckwith Major 144,145,148
Behrens Lt. 172,177
Besika Bay 185
Birdwood Lt General 28
Birkett Captain 177
Bishop Major 82,84,88
Black Sea 8,25
Blake Lt RAMC 172
Bolton Captain 95
Bonaparte Napoleon 7
Braithwaite Major General 34
Bromley Captain C VC 84,90,103,105,106
Bulair 185,186
Carden Admiral S 27,28,31,33,34
Carr Major 93
Carrington Smith Lt. Colonel N141,142,143
Casson Lt Colonel HG 169,171,172,174,175,176,
  178,179
Casualties British :
  Y Beach 55,56,58
  W Beach 100
  V Beach 131,154
  S 177
  Total 25-30 April 187
Cayley Colonel 99
Cemeteries: (Commonwealth War Graves
Commission):
  Cannakale Consular 16
  Lancashire Landing 22,89,114,115,143
  Pink Farm 21,73,77,79
  Redoubt 24,97
  Twelve Tree Copse 21,56,77,79
  Solitary grave of Lt. Colonel Doughty Wylie:
    23,155,160,161,162,163,164
  Skew Bridge 24,181
  V Beach 135,147,150,155,157

Memorials:
  Helles Memorial 8,10,17,21,22,23,25,91,100,
    115,117,140,155,168,172,174
  Seaford 106
  Other Cemeteries/Memorials
    French 182,183
    Turkish 61,62,157,184
Chamberlain Lt. 177
Cheatle Lt WJN 56
Churchill Major J 42,43
Churchill W First Lord of the Admiralty
  28,32,33,34,36,43
Clayton Captain 89
Cooper Captain AS 48
Cosgrove Cpl W VC 147,148
Costeker Captain JHD 93,142
Cunliffe-Owen Lt Colonel 36
Dardanelles 8,17, **25-42**
Davidson Captain A HMS Cornwallis 172
De Tott's Batery 167,172,174,178
Dodge Lt J 132
Doughty Wylie Lt Colonel CHM VC 6,23,58,145,148,149
Drewry Midshipman GL VC 124,135,136,137,138,139
Duckworth Admiral 25
Enver Pasha Turkish Minister of War 25
Faussett Lt Colonel OG Godfrey DSO 93,97
Farmar Captain 91,92,96
Finn Rev. Father WJ 134,135
Fisher Lord First Sea Lord 26
Forester Flet Surgeon RN 71
Forts:
  No.3 (Old Fort) 23,33,120,121,122, 137,143,145,
    146,148,150
  No. 1 23,32,99,120,121,122,145
Frankland Major THC 70,90,91,92
Freyberg Lt Commander BC 187
Geddes Captain GW 122,136,137
Grimshaw Major CTW 148,149,150
Grimshaw L/Cpl JE VC 102,103,107,108
Guezji Baba 91,97,98,99
Hamilton General Sir I34,35,36,37,38,42,47,48,
  54,65,68,93,101,102,120,122,126,143,167,176
Hankey Colonel Sir M 33
Hare Brigadier General 45,67,70,82,91,99,123,125
Haworth Captain 84,91,96,102
Helles 8,10,17,21,25
Henderson Captain 136,137
Hills:
  114 22,64,69,70,80,81,84,90,92,93,95,99,144,
  141 22,23,73,75,91,102,120,121,144,145,146,
    147,148,149,150,178
  138 22,73,74,75,81,84,90,91,93,95,97,99,102,144
  236 175
  Achi Baba 24,41,43,45,52,100,141,149,151,176,178
  Observation 24
Hope Captain DW 31,32
Hunter Weston Major General A
  28,48,54,55,92,102,126,148,150,151,178,180
James Lt. DA 71,73
Jarrett Major CHB 58, 141,143

190

Johnson Captain DD 177
Jones Lt Colonel F 73
Keneally L/Sgt W VC 102,104,105
Keyes Commodore R 31,34
Kitchener Lord 27, 28,35
Koe Lt Colonel AS 43,45,50,55
Krithia 13,18,21,24,43,48,64,91,140,151,179
Lemnos/Mudros Harbour 35,37,38,65,66,
    81,82,123,125,126,169
Leslie Captain 69
Limpus Admiral 26
Lockyer Captain H RN 67
Lough Captain 49, 54
Maffett Lt 132
Malleson Midshipman W VC 135,138,139
Margesson Major EC 171,173,177
Marrow Captain EA 56
Marshall Brigadier General 69,70,71,73,74
Matthews Lt Colonel GE 33,4345,48,50,51,
    52,54,55,56,57
Maunsell Captain TB 89
Maxwell General 28
McAlester Major WHS 48,56,57
McKenzie Samson Seaman G VC 135,136,139
Meatyard Sgt. W 51

Military Forces:
British:
    Divisions:
        29th 32,37,40,41,45,55,64,66,69,81, 95,99,
            100,120,123,150,151,154,168,176
        Royal Naval 37,38,41,126,132,168,179,186
        Royal Naval Armoured Car Division 125
    Brigades:
        86 50,123
        87 74,154,179
        88 102
        157 179
    Infantry Battalions
        Anson RND 64,70,92,129,130
        1/Border 64,69,70,71,72,73,74,142
        1/Essex 92,93,95,97,99,141,142
        2/Hampshire 93,95,99,142,143
        1/Kings Own Scottish Borderers
            43,46,48,50,51,55,56,58,59,70
        l/Lancashire Fusiliers 48,64,67,81,82, 85,86,
            88,90,92,93,95,96,97,100,101,102
        RMLI Plymouth 43,46,59
        1/Royal Dublin Fusiliers 93,129,130,131,134,137
        2/Royal Fusiliers 64,67,69,70,71,73,81,
            84,92,93,95
        1/Royal Iniskilling Fusiliers 64,69,70,73
        1/Royal Munster Fusiliers 130,135,136,141
        1/5 Royal Scots 93,123
        2/South Wales Borderers 50,53,58,59,
            70,154,167,168,169,175,176,178
        4/Worcesters 93,95,96,97,98,99,102,142,143
    Air Service
        Royal Naval Air Service 125,142
    Engineers:
        Royal Engineers 123

2/ London Field Coy 92
Army Service Corps
    Army Service Corps 123

French: 151,154,167,178
Turkish: 41,49,51,68,69,84,123,172,177

Millward L.Cpl. 180
Morse Lt 137,138
Morto Bay 167,170
Morton Captain 71
Napier Brigadier General HE 58,93,142
Newenham Lt Colonel 69,70,73,90,91
Nightingale Lt G 58, 141,143
Ogilvy Captain GMH 48
Order of Battle: 42
Ormond Lt Colonel 81,82
Palmer Captain R G 43,58
Ray Captain ADH 97
Raymond E 108,187
Richards Sgt A VC 102,103,104
de Robeck Rear Admiral JM 29,34,36
Robinson Lt Commander EG 32
RoothLt Colonel RA 131,134,135,144
Sami Bey Colonel 51
Samson Lt Commander 138
Sedd El Bahr 23,127,129,137,141,144,145,146,148,
    150,168,175,176,178
Shaw Captain 84,88,91,93

Ships
    Bouvet (Fr) 35
    Gaulois (Fr) 36
    Souffren (Fr) 36
    Askold (R) 168,170
    SS *Alaunia* 169
    HMS *Albion* 127
    HMS *Amethyst* 46,53
    SS *Andania* 64,69
    HMT *Ansonia* 59
    HT *Caledonia* 81
    SS *Canada* 169
    HMS *Cornwallis* 43,66,82,126,137,169
    HMS *Dartmouth* 186
    HMS *Doris* 186
    Duke of Edinburgh 64,69
    HMS *Dublin* 54,127
    HMS *Euraylus* 45,66,82,85,92,101,126
    HMS *Fearless* 68
    HMS *Goliath* 46,59,127
    HMS *Hussar* 123
    HMS *Implacable* 48,66,67,68,69,70,71,82,84,126
    HMS *Inflexible* 31, 36
    HNS *Irresistible* 32,36
    HMS *Lord Nelson* 127
    HMS *Minerva* 127
    Minesweeper No. 6 69
    HMS *Ocean* 36
    HMS *Prince George* 127
    HMS *Queen Elizabeth* 31,32,34,36,38,4248,
        54,126,141

191

SS *River Clyde* 66,82,93,119,122,123,124,125, 130, 134,135,136,139,140,141,142,143, 144,145,165
HMS *Sapphire* 46,52,53
HMS *Swiftsure* 85,127
HMS *Talbot* 127
HMS *Triumph* 169
HMS *Vengeance* 31,32,127
Transport No. 2 46
Transport Aragon 93
Transport Dongola 93
Transport Manitou 169
Fleetsweeper No 1 66
HMS *Irresistible* 32,36

Submarines
E15 32
Souchon Admiral 26
Stirling-Cookson Lt CS 46
Stubbs Sgt FE VC 102,103,107
Talaat Bey 25
Tisdall Sb,Lt. A VC 135,140

Tizard Lt Colonel 133,144,145
Tours/Walks:
Orientation 18-24
Y Beach 59-63
X Beach 76-79
W Beach 109-118
V Beach 155 165
S Beach 181-184

Unwin Commander E 123,124,135,136,137,139
Vaughan Major CD 72,73
Von Sanders General Liman 26,29
Walford Captain GN VC 145,146,150
Ward Lt 93
Wedgewood Commander J 125,141
Welch Major A 46,48,52
Wemyss Rear Admiral 123,124
Williams Orlo CCO 126,188
Williams Lt Colonel Weir de Lancy Williams 130,145
Williams Able Seaman WC VC 135,136,137
Willis Captain R VC 84,86,87,88,88,89,92,102,103
Wolley Dod Colonel 96,98,99,103

ACKNOWLEDGEMENTS

After frequent visits to the battlefields of the Gallipoli Peninsula over several years, it has been a great opportunity to be able to tell the story of the landings at Helles in some detail. However this could not have been done without the valued assistance of such organisations as the Public Records Office, Kew, and the invaluable and patient help of the Regimental Museum Secretaries, Curators and Archivists. The use of Regimental histories and records, war diaries and personal diaries has enabled an accurate picture as possible to emerge. In particular for permission to use extracts from regimental histories, contemporary sketches, maps and photographs, we would like to thank Col. Peter Crocker Royal Welch Fusiliers Regimental Museum, Ian Hook, Essex Regiment Museum Chelmsford, The Bursar, Ushaw College Durham, Ian Martin, The King's Own Scottish Borderers Regimental Museum, Stuart Eastwood Border Regiment Museum, The Royal Regiment of Fusiliers (City of London) Museum, Lancashire Fusiliers Museum Bury, Major R Prophet Worcestershire Regiment Museum, Major Jack Dunlop Royal Inniskilling Fusiliers, Mr T. Moloney Royal Munster Fusiliers, Mr.Little Royal Marines Museum, Colonel Keating Royal Hampshire Regiment Museum, Major M Everett Museums of the Royal Regiment of Wales (24th/41st Foot). Schull Books for extracts from Neill's Blue Caps the history of the Royal Dublin Fusiliers, and Mme Stocanne President Association Nationale pour le Souvenir des Dardanelles. We would also warmly thank Brian Head, Archivist at the Royal Navy Submarine Museum, Gosport for his great help and the benefit of his extensive knowledge together with the Keeper of Records for great assistance with our enquiries.

We are grateful to the Commonwealth War Graves Commission for their permission to reproduce their map and for their unfailing courtesy in all our dealings with them. Despite the trying conditions of searing heat in summer and bitterly cold weather in winter, the work of the gardeners goes on, and in Spring particularly, the flowers and trees in each provide a spectacular and fitting setting for the graves of the men who remain on the Peninsula.

But such an undertaking as this could not have been done without the cheerful support and encouragement of those stalwart friends of ours who have trod many a battlefield with us, including Gallipoli. We would especially thank Michael and Rita Clarke, for use of some excellent modern day photographs, and Eric Lewis, Doug Sim, Ann Warren, and Sian Johnston (nee Rodge) for chasing around the UK on our behalf taking further pictures. Mrs. Pat Evans has proved indefatigable in her assistance over the years on the finer points of the Campaign, also Ron Sparkes for his help on Ernest Raymond. We also very much appreciate the practical advice and willing help given by fellow author Dr.Graham Keech, the support of Nevin Anthony in our initial ventures onto the Peninsula, and the advice and encouragement of Major Toni and Mrs. Valmai Holt in the writing of this book and to Nigel Cave for his help as Series Editor.